# THE BEST OF SYDNEY

# THE BEST OF
## *Sydney*

NH
NEW
HOLLAND

# Contents

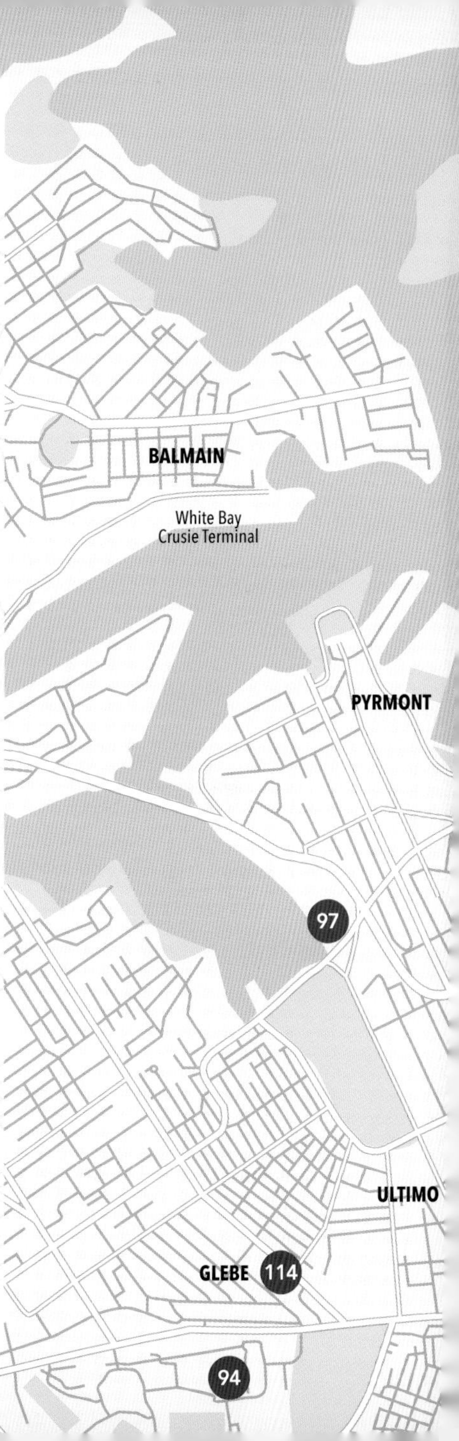
112
BALMAIN
White Bay
Crusie Terminal
PYRMONT
97
99
ULTIMO
GLEBE
114
94



Note: Blue numbers also refer to page numbers

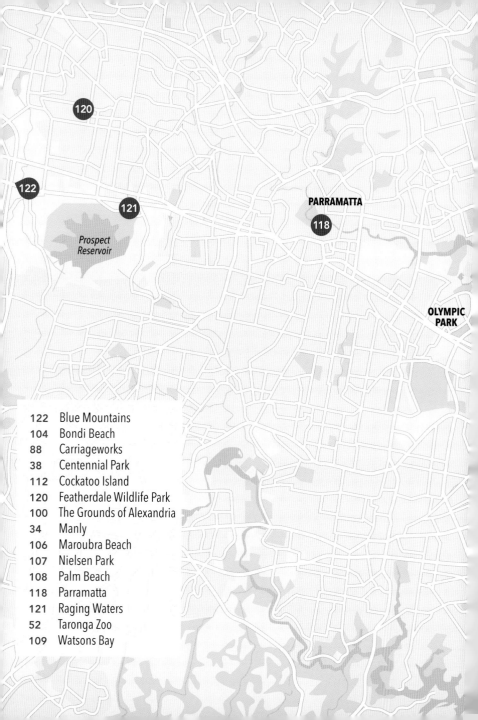

**PARRAMATTA**

**OLYMPIC PARK**

*Prospect Reservoir*

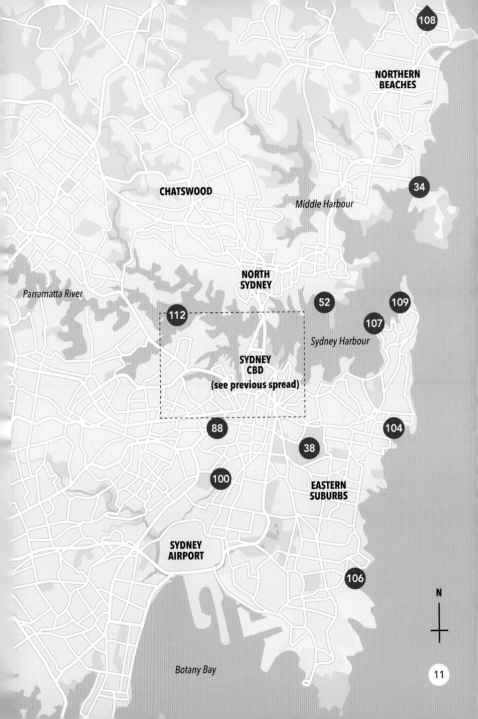

NORTHERN
BEACHES

108

CHATSWOOD

34

Middle Harbour

NORTH
SYDNEY

Parramatta River

52

109

112

107

Sydney Harbour

SYDNEY
CBD
(see previous spread)

88

104

38

100

EASTERN
SUBURBS

SYDNEY
AIRPORT

106

N

Botany Bay

# Welcome to Sydney!

Sydney is Australia's oldest city. Its birthday is 26 January 1788. It started off as a prison for people so poor that they had to steal to survive, and if they got caught the British government of the time sent them halfway across the world to stake a claim on imperial real estate. Eventually most of these prisoners served their time and many who stayed became very rich, becoming the ancestors of founding families of what would eventually become the nation of Australia. Many of them even had suburbs named after them. The first colonists were English, Irish and Scots, and a considerable number of Chinese also settled there.

Sydney is located in the state of New South Wales, which covers an area of 809,444 square kilometres (312,528 square miles) or, to put it into perspective, roughly about the size of Texas and most of Louisiana combined, or, to put it another way, larger than two Germanies or two Japans. New South Wales is roughly divided in half by the Great Dividing Range. The western half of New South Wales is arid to desert, while the eastern half, where most people live, has an oceanic to subtropical climate and much better soil.

As a special bonus the one thing that overseas visitors find remarkable about not only Sydney, but all the cities of Australia, is the profusion of wildlife, especially bird life. Australians are never very far away from nature, which contributes to the status that Australian cities consistently have of being some of the most livable cities in the world, as well as some of the prettiest.

## The People of Sydney

The first human inhabitants of the region now occupied by the central business district of Sydney were the Gadigal people of the Eora nation, who have been here, literally, since time immemorial.

After World War II, Australia decided that there was a lot of work to be done and Australians weren't breeding fast enough to do it all, so we started importing people in considerable quantities. Many of them stayed in Sydney and as a result this city of over 4.5 million is one of the most culturally and linguistically diverse in the world.

Some of the more significant populations of Sydneysiders who weren't born in Australia include people from China, the United Kingdom, India, New Zealand, Vietnam, the Philippines, South Korea, Lebanon, Hong Kong, Italy, Iraq, South Africa, Fiji and Greece.

Sydney Town Hall

Sydney is also the highest-ranking city in the world for international students with about 100,000 studying either at university, vocational colleges or English language schools.

As a result of all this diversity, visiting Sydney is a little like visiting the world in miniature and, depending on where you go, you're likely to bump into a variety of people from different backgrounds and walks of life.

## Sydney's Personality

One of Australia's most well-known playwrights, David Williamson, wrote a play that's loosely about Sydney in which one character describes the city as 'New York without the intellect'. This is a bit harsh, but it remains true that even though Sydney is Australia's oldest city, its personality is that of a brash youngster, up-and-coming, on the make, ready to do a deal. Visitors to the city generally find that the people are friendly, if a little hurried, because they've got a lot on.

## What Sydney Has That Other Places Don't Have

The jewel of Sydney is its harbor. Even when it was first seen by Europeans, mariners described it as one of the best natural harbors in the world. It's still a major center for commercial shipping, but while container traffic has moved south to Botany Bay, Sydney Harbour now plays host to cruise ships from all over the world as well as first-class yachts. Even the mundanity of commuting is something special for many Sydneysiders who take advantage of the ferry system, which services jetties as far apart as Parramatta in the west and Manly in the north-east. So the first thing that visitors to Sydney usually want to see is the harbor and its foreshore and the variety of attractions it has to offer.

Having said that, Sydney is a big city and there are a lot of interesting things to do and places to visit outside of the central business district. There's enough here to suit almost everyone, and, as an added bonus, you don't have to spend much money in Sydney to have a great time.

Of course, you're free to splurge too.

## Getting Around

Sydney has an excellent public transport system. Ticketing is centralized through a system called Opal card, which can be used on buses, trains, ferries and light rail. You can get Opal cards from most newsagents and convenience stores. Opal cards can be topped up online, over the  counter at Opal retailers, or at some transport customer service centers. When using public transport, you need to tap on when you board and tap off when you arrive at your stop. If you are transferring to another service, you need to tap on again and tap off at your destination.

There is no charge for an Opal card, however the minimum value is $10 for an adult Opal card and $5 for a child/youth Opal card. At Sydney Airport stations a minimum top-up of $35 applies.

If you don't have an Opal card, contactless payments are available with compatible payment cards or mobile devices on most train, ferry and light rail services and will be equivalent to a standard (peak) adult Opal fare in most cases.

For further information visit: **www.transportnsw.info/tickets-opal/opal/opal-for-visitors**.

Maps of the Sydney public transport network are available from most train stations or online at: **www.transportnsw.info/routes/train** and that site will get you access to information about bus, ferry and light rail services too. Alternatively, you can call 131 500.

Sydney's main transport hubs are Central Station, Town Hall, Circular Quay and Parramatta. All references to 'How to get there' in this book use Central Station as a starting reference point.

## Big Bus Sydney Hop-On, Hop-Off Bus

The Big Bus Sydney hop-on hop-off bus is a great way to experience all the main sights of Sydney if you don't have a lot of time or just want to get your bearings. This open-top double-decker bus tours operate two routes: the Sydney tour (Red route) and the Bondi Tour (Blue route). The buses run every 15–20 minutes and you can buy tickets that are valid for 24 or 48 hours. An audio commentary in eight different languages is also available.

Tickets: Adults $55/$75, Children (5–15) $38/$50, Family (2 adults + 2 children) $148/$200

Website: **www.theaustralianexplorer.com.au/sydney-bondi-explorer**

## Going Your Own Way

If you want to go your own way there are a number of rent-a-car companies, including all the major international chains, and yes, Sydney also has Uber services.

Sydney is a world-class city with a highly developed infrastructure and services, but you'll still have problems getting a cab on a Friday or Saturday night if you don't book ahead.

## *Sydney Taxi Cab Numbers*

| | |
|---|---|
| Australia Wide Taxis | 131 008 |
| 13cabs | 132 227 |
| Legion Cabs | 131 451 |
| Silver Service Cabs | 133 100 |
| Premier Cabs | 131 017 |
| Premier Prestige Cabs | 132 824 |
| RSL Cabs | 02 9581 1111 |
| RSL Prestige Bookings | 02 9470 1100 |

Prestige services get you a better type of limousine-style cab, when the occasion calls for it.

Many cab companies offer minibus services if you need to book a cab for more than four people and can also provide baby seats or cabs that can take wheelchairs. Just let them know at the time that you book. For wheelchair taxis call Zero200 on 02 8332 0200.

In Australia, it is considered polite for at least one passenger to sit up front with the driver, unless you're only traveling as a couple. It's part of our tradition of egalitarianism, which we still pay a lot of lip service to.

## Tourist Information Offices

The hub of visitor information for Sydney is **www.sydney.com**.

There are several information centers within the Sydney metropolitan area but Sydney and Manly are the most popular.

For the Sydney Visitor Centre, see **The Rocks** (page 26).

For the Manly Visitor Information Centre, see **Manly** (page 34).

# Must-sees

Every city in Australia has a list of their must-see attractions, and while what is and isn't on a list depends on who you talk to and how long that list is, there are always a few attractions that should be on everyone's list. Here's our list of Sydney must-sees.

## Sydney Harbour Bridge

Why you should go:  Because it's famous.  Because you see it every year on television when it turns into the world's largest New Year's fireworks display.  Because you can walk across it on the east side and bicycle across on the west side.  Because it offers a marvelous and unique view of the city from high up in the center of the harbor without having to rent a helicopter.

How to get there:  Best get a map at the **Sydney Visitors Centre in the Rocks** (page 26) because you could get lost in the maze of ancient streets.

Time:  One to two hours depending on how leisurely you want to take it.

How much? FREE! Unless you want to visit the **Pylon Lookout** which has an information center and takes you even

higher up. Opening hours: 10.00 am to 5.00 pm seven days; General admission $15 (13 years and over), concessions $10, children $8.50, under 4 years free; Website: **www.pylonlookout.com.au**.

If you're feeling really adventurous and energetic and you have the budget you can do the **BridgeClimb**, which actually takes you onto the upper structure of the bridge itself. Adults (16 and up) $174–$388, children (8 to 15) $148–$278. Phone: 02 8274 7777 for bookings or go online: **www.bridgeclimb.com**.

For the virtual visitor: The Sydney Harbour Bridge self-guided walking tour available as an MP3 download: $10 **www.selfguidedwalkingtours.com/walks/SydneyHarbourBridge.php**.

While you're in the area: Include this as part of your visit to **The Rocks** (page 26) or **Luna Park** (page 51).

## Sydney Opera House

Why you should go:  Because it's one of the world's most famous buildings.  At the time it was built it was also one of the most controversial.  The Danish architect Jørn Utzon, who won the international competition for its design, argued so much with Davis Hughes, the New South Wales minister for public arts who 'had no interest in art, architecture or aesthetics', that he left Sydney and never returned, dying at age 90 without ever seeing the building that made him famous.  Anyway, you couldn't possibly visit Sydney without visiting the Opera House.  Your friends would never forgive you.

Phone: 02 9250 7111

Website: **www.sydneyoperahouse.com**

How to get there:  Catch the train to Circular Quay and stroll north-east for 10 minutes.  You can actually see it from the station.  It sticks out like a brilliantly designed sore thumb.

Opening hours:  You can visit the outside at any time.

Time budget:  At least an hour.

How much? FREE! But the Opera House is also a multi-venue space that hosts exhibitions, theatrical plays, concerts and, of course, opera, and tickets can range from around $20 to hundreds of dollars depending on the event and seating. You could easily plan a whole day there if there's a lot on that suits your taste.  Hour-long standard tours run daily between 9.00 am and 5.00 pm and cost $42 per person.  Backstage tours run daily at 7.00 am and cost $175 per person.  Access tours for people with mobility issues are also available at 12.00 pm daily.

While you're in the area:  You could eat at **Bennelong** restaurant (page 139) or **Opera Kitchen** (page 139) which are both right on site, or take a short walk to **Aria** restaurant (page 138).  You could wander through the **Royal Botanic Gardens** (page 33) to the immediate east and further south-east to the **Art Gallery of New South Wales** (page 29), or you can walk west to Circular Quay and keep going west to **The Rocks** (page 26).

# The Rocks

Why you should go: Because it's the historic heart of Sydney and includes many of its oldest surviving buildings. The Rocks has more than 50 cafes, restaurants and hotels to eat and drink in and as many shops, ranging from cheap and cheerful souvenirs to high-end boutiques and everything in between.

How to get there: From Central Station catch a train to Circular Quay Station. From there it's a 10-minute slow stroll to The Rocks, on the west side of Circular Quay.

Time budget: Several hours.

**Sydney Visitor Centre – The Rocks:** Shop 1–2, 12–24 Playfair Street (corner of Playfair Street and Argyle Street) Opening hours: 9.30 am to 5.30 pm seven days; Phone: 1800 067 676 (free call), 02 8273 0000; Website: **www.therocks.com**.

**The Rocks Discovery Museum:** The Rocks Discovery Museum is a free, family-friendly museum housed in a restored 1850s sandstone warehouse which tells the story of The Rocks area from pre-European days to the present. The museum is home to interactive exhibits and a collection of Rocksian images and archaeological artifacts. Address: Kendall Lane (enter via Argyle Street), The Rocks; Open: 10.00 am to 5.00 pm daily; Admission: Free; Phone: 02 9240 8680; Website: **www.therocks.com/things-to-do/the-rocks-discovery-museum.aspx**.

**Susannah Place Museum:** This terrace house, built in 1844, demonstrates how people lived in the area from the early years of colonial settlement on with re-created interiors that tell the real stories of the people who called Susannah Place home. Address: 58–64 Gloucester Street, The Rocks; Opening hours: Daily 2.00 pm to 5.00 pm with access by guided tour only, last tour leaving at 4 pm; Admission: Adults $12,

concessions $8, families $30, children under five free; Phone: 02 9241 1893; Website: **www.sydneylivingmuseums.com.au/ susannah-place-museum**.

**The Rocks Walking Tours:** A great way to explore the area while learning more about its fascinating history. Address: Clocktower Square, Shop 4a, Cnr Argyle and Harrington streets, The Rocks; Tours depart daily at 10.30 am and 1.30 pm and take 90 minutes; Adults $32, children (5–16 years) $15, children under 5 free, family $79, concessions/backpackers $25; Phone: 02 9247 6678; Website: **www.rockswalkingtours.com.au**.

**The Rocks Market:** This makers' market operates on Saturdays and Sundays from 10.00 am to 5.00 pm, Playfair Street, George Street and Jack Mundey Place, The Rocks.

**Bonza Bike Tours:** Fun and interesting bike tours of Sydney; Address: 30 Harrington Street, The Rocks; Phone: 02 9247 8800; Website: **www.bonzabiketours.com**.

**Paniq Room:** An experiential escape game; Phone: 0414 468 430; Website: **www.paniqroom.com.au**.

**Silent Disco Tours:** Phone: 0416 210 187; Website: **www.discotours.com.au**.

**Rocks Photography Tour:** Tour The Rocks with a professional photographer; Phone 02 9427 9636; Website: **www.sydneyphotographytours.com**.

While you're in the area: It's only a short stroll to the entrance to the walkways on the Harbour Bridge but be prepared to climb a lot of stairs. If you go past the bridge and keep walking west you'll come to the **Barangaroo Reserve** (page 31). Walking east will take you to Circular Quay and then on to the **Sydney Opera House** (page 24). **Sydney Observatory** (page 82) and the **Museum of Contemporary Art** (page 65) are also in the area.

## Art Gallery of New South Wales

Why you should go: For the art, for the beautiful building and for the location on the edge of **The Domain** and the **Royal Botanic Gardens.** Established in 1871 the Art Gallery of New South Wales is still one of the largest and most important galleries in Australia. Its collections include Aboriginal and Torres Strait Islander art, modern and contemporary works, a distinguished

collection of colonial and nineteenth-century Australian works and European old masters.

Address:  Art Gallery Road, The Domain 2000

Phone: 1800 679 278 (free call)

Website: **www.artgallery.nsw.gov.au**

How to get there:  Catch the train to either St James Station or Martin Place Station and walk east for about 10 minutes.  It's at the eastern end of a park called **The Domain**.  Ask a friendly local;  you can't miss it.  You can also catch the 441 bus from the York Street side of the **Queen Victoria Building** (page 68) which is just near Town Hall Station.

Opening hours: 10.00 am to 5.00 pm seven days, every Wednesday is Art After Hours and the gallery stays open until 10.00 pm.

Time budget: Three hours.

How much? FREE! Yep, general admission doesn't cost a cent but donations are always welcome and generate good karma.  General admission allows you to see the permanent galleries and most temporary exhibitions.  Special exhibitions generally cost from around $20 for adults, $18 seniors and concession, $8 children (17 and under), $50 for families (2 adults and up to 3 children).

While you're in the area:  If the weather is good, stroll north to the **Royal Botanic Gardens**.  If you're hungry and in the mood for Asian fine dining, take a short walk east to **China Doll** restaurant (page 140) at Woolloomooloo.  The art gallery has a cafe for light meals and snacks and **Chiswick at the Gallery** for à la carte meals.

# Barangaroo Reserve and Dining Precinct

Why you should go:  To see how the site of a former concrete container terminal has been turned into nature reserve, smack bang in the middle of a major city, planted with more than 75,000 native trees and shrubs.  The Barangaroo precinct also includes office towers and a wide range of shops and restaurants at the southern end of the site.

Address:  It's a whole area unto itself, 1 kilometre (about ½ a mile) west of the Sydney CBD

Phone: 02 9255 1700  or 1300 966 480 (after hours)

Website: **www.barangaroo.com**

How to get there: Catch the train to Circular Quay and walk west or catch the ferry that will take you directly to Barangaroo Wharf and walk north.

Time budget:  Two hours.

How much? FREE! Unless you want to take one of the highly recommended **Aboriginal Cultural Tours** that happen every morning at 10.30, Monday through to Saturday:  Adults $36.50, seniors and concessions $22, children $16.50.  Book online: **www.barangaroo.com/see-and-do/things-to-do/tours/aboriginal-cultural-tours**.

While you're in the area:  Keep walking south and explore the Barangaroo urban redevelopment precinct.  There are dozens of options for drinking and dining from cafes and bars to fine dining, including **Bea Restaurant** (page 139) at **Barangaroo House**.  If you keep walking, you'll seamlessly stroll into **Darling Harbour** (page 40).

# Royal Botanic Gardens

Why you should go: There are 30 hectares (74 acres) of trees and plants from all over the world that can grow in Sydney's subtropical climate and have been doing their thing for over 200 years. It's one of the few botanical gardens in the world that has a harbor view, and a lovely place to have a picnic.

Address: Mrs Macquaries Road, Sydney 2000 (just east of the Opera House and stretching south to The Domain)

Phone: 02 9231 8111

Website: **www.rbgsyd.nsw.gov.au**

How to get there: Catch the train to Circular Quay and walk towards the **Sydney Opera House**. There is an entrance near the south-east corner of the Opera House. If coming from the city you can also enter via Macquarie Street.

Opening hours: Opens every day at 7.00 am, closes around 5.00 pm in the colder months (April to September) and 6.00 pm to 8.00 pm in the warmer months (October to March).

Time budget: Two to three hours.

How much? FREE! Unless you want to take one of the highly recommended Aboriginal Heritage Tours that happen every morning from 10.00 am to 11.30 am on Wednesdays, Fridays and Saturdays (excluding public holidays); $41 per person, children 7 years and under free; book online: **www.rbgsyd.nsw.gov.au/whatson/Aboriginal-Heritage-Tour.** There are also special events running all year round so it's worth visiting the website to see what's on.

While you're in the area: To the immediate west is the **Sydney Opera House**, and to the immediate south is **The Domain** and the **Art Gallery of New South Wales** (pages 29–30). Also try the **Australian Bush Food** experience (page 143).

# Manly

Why you should go:  To see a different, more leisurely, side of Sydney that's still easily accessible.  Manly has a fine beach and has been a destination for surfers since the 1960s, but for many the real fun is the **ferry ride** that shows off the harbor.  You will find more than 200 boutiques and specialty shops in Manly and more than 100 restaurants and cafes.

**Manly Visitor Information Centre**, Many Wharf Forecourt, East Esplanade, Manly;  Phone: 02 9976 1430;  Website: **www.hellomanly.com.au**;  Opening hours: 9.00 am to 5.00 pm Monday to Friday, 10.00 am to 4.00 pm weekends and public holidays.

How to get there:  From Central Station catch a train to Circular Quay.  From there the best was to get to Manly is by **ferry** from Wharf F1.  The ferry usually leaves on the hour and half hour and travel time between Circular Quay and Manly is 30 minutes or thereabouts.  If you're in a hurry, you can catch the **Manly Jetcat** which takes 15 minutes each way.

Time budget:  At least four hours.

How much? FREE!

Manly is a whole suburb that you can explore.  Some highlights include:

**The Manly Beach/Cabbage Tree Bay coastal walk**:  There are also another 17 beaches to visit.

**Manly Market Place** selling arts and crafts on Saturday and Sunday (weather permitting) and **Manly Fresh** to find fresh produce on Sundays, in Sydney Road, Manly.

**North Head Tunnel Tour:**  Guided tour through World War II tunnels that runs on Sundays.  Address:  North Fort Visitors Centre, North Head Scenic Drive, Manly;

Cost: Adults $7, children (under 16), pensioners and concessions $5, families (2 adults and up to 3 children) $20; Website: **www.harbourtrust.gov.au**.

**Ghost Tours of the Quarantine Station:** Address: 1 North Head Scenic Drive, Manly; Hours: 8 pm nightly and 5.30 pm Saturdays; Cost: Adults $49 weekdays $55 Saturdays; concessions $44 weekdays $49 Saturdays; Phone: 02 9466 1500; Website: **www.qstation.com.au/ghost-tours**.

**Taronga Zoo Combo:** Includes admission to Taronga Zoo and a 24-hour Eco Hopper hop-on hop-off pass with 10 top locations, including Taronga Zoo, Manly and Q Station. Adults $65, children $39; Website: **www.thesydneypass.com** or can be booked through the Manly Visitor Information Centre.

While you're in the area: Stay there because you can easily spend the whole day, there's so much to experience!

# Fun with the Kids

Some attractions are more child friendly that others while others are specifically designed to appeal to the under 18s, especially if your kids are really young. Here are some places to visit that you can bring the whole family to that have gone that extra mile to keep the kiddies entertained.

# Centennial Park and the Ian Potter Children's Wild Play Garden

Why you should go:  Because you get to see a lovely part of Sydney – 'the lungs of the city' – within a short bus ride of the CBD.  It's a great place to visit if you just want a restful, picniccy type day and the Children's Wild Play Garden is a lot of fun for both kids and grown-ups.

Address:  It's the size of a whole suburb, 3 kilometres (about 1½ miles) south-east of the Sydney CBD

Website: **www.centennialparklands.com.au**

How to get there:  Catch the 333 bus from the city up Oxford Street and get off at Centennial Square (about 20 minutes).

Opening hours:  In the colder months (April to October) the park is open every day from around 6.30 am to 5.30 pm and in the warmer months (November to March) from around 6.00 am to 8.00 pm.  The **Visitor Information Counter** is located at the corner of Grand Drive and Parkes Drive and is open from 9 am to 4 pm Monday to Friday and 9 am to 2 pm on weekends.  The Ian Potter Children's Wild Play Garden is open from 10.00 am to 5.00 pm daily.

Time budget:  Two hours or more.

How much? FREE! But there are also some fun paid events like the Spotlight Prowls, occasional Aboriginal art, craft and food classes, and Astronomy 101.  Visit the website for more details.  During the warmer months you can catch a movie outdoors at the **Moonlight Cinema** (**www.moonlight.com.au**).

While you're in the area: Wander the streets of Paddington, lined with Victorian terrace house or you could get back on the bus on Oxford Street and continue on to **Bondi Beach** (page 104).

# Darling Harbour and the Darling Quarter Playground

Why you should go: Because it's fun and makes for a great urban walk. There is a huge range of eateries and shops, and it's also centrally located to a lot of other attractions. The playground is a large area entirely designed for the young and the young at heart to have fun in. It can get really crowded on weekends, so, if you can, visit it on a weekday. It's at its most fun in the height of summer when you can take your shoes off, roll up your trousers and, well, splash around a bit with the wee ones.

Address: Just a short walk west of the CBD down King or Market Streets.

Websites: **www.darlingharbour.com**; **www.darlingquarter.com**

How to get there: There are so many ways to get to Darling Harbour that you're spoiled for choice. Arguably the most pleasant and simplest is to catch the light rail from Central, alight at Convention Centre and walk east.

Opening hours: Open all the time.

Time budget: Two hours or more.

How much? FREE! Or spend as much as you like in the shops and other attractions.

While you're in the area: Darling Harbour is home to the following attractions:

- **Madame Tussauds** (page 42)
- **The Australian National Maritime Museum** (page 60) and the Sydney Heritage Fleet (**www.shf.org.au**)
- **SEA LIFE Sydney Aquarium** (page 44)

If you like high-end Chinese food in an elegant setting try the **Blue Eye Dragon** restaurant (page 139).

## FOUR ATTRACTIONS PASS

The best value deal if you want to see a lot at Darling Harbour is a four-attractions package which gives you admission to:

- Madame Tussauds
- SEA LIFE Sydney Aquarium
- The Sydney Tower Eye
- WILD LIFE Sydney Zoo

… and a narrated city tour on the Big Bus, which is available in multiple languages.  That deal costs $99 for adults and $70 for kids and represents considerable (over 50%) savings. Best to visit **www.sydneytowereye.com.au/tickets** or any of the other websites of these attractions for details.

## Madame Tussauds

Why you should go: Because seeing lifelike wax facsimiles is about as close as most of us ever get to encountering celebrities and is pretty much your only option if you want to 'meet' long-dead historical figures. It's also fun comparing how close the figures are to the real thing.

Address: 1–5 Wheat Road, Sydney 2000 (right next to SEA LIFE Aquarium in Darling Harbour)

Website: **www.madametussauds.com.au**

How to get there: So easy! It's just a short stroll west of the CBD down King or Market streets.

Opening hours: 10.00 am to 5.00 pm seven days.

Time budget: Two to three hours.

How much? Depending on what you want to see, some visits have to be booked. Prices start from $35 for general admission or do the **Four Attractions Pass** (page 41).

While you're in the area: There's the **SEA LIFE Aquarium** (page 44) and the **WILD LIFE Sydney Zoo** (page 55). The **Barangaroo Reserve** (page 31) is just north, and to the south is the rest of **Darling Harbour** (page 40).

# Pineapple's Pirates on Sydney Harbour

Why you should go:  Because it's the most fun you'll have with your inner pirate this side of the Caribbean.  See the harbor while pretending to be a pirate on a genuine tall sailing ship.  Guaranteed to shiver your timbers.

Address:  Campbells Cove Pontoon, Circular Quay or Ives Step Wharf at the tip of Dawes Point or another nearby wharf, depending on the day

Phone: 02 8015 5571

Website: **www.sydneytallships.com.au**

How to get there:  So easy! Catch a train or walk to Circular Quay then walk north up the west side of the Quay, past the Overseas Passenger Terminal.  Tall Ships emails you a map on booking because departure points sometimes vary slightly.

Opening hours:  Boarding at 11.45 am for the cruise which departs at 12.00 pm and finishes about 1.30 pm every day.

Time budget:  At least two hours.

How much? $54 per person but the best value deal is the family pass, 2 adults 2 children for $162.  Nice add-ons include the Mast Climb Challenge for $30 per person and the drinks package at $28 per person.

While you're in the area: Visit **The Rocks** (page 26), the **Museum of Contemporary Art** (page 65) or take a walk on the **Harbour Bridge** (page 22).

## SEA LIFE Sydney Aquarium

Why you should go:  Because where else will you get to see such a
profusion of oceanic life without actually getting wet, or seasick,
or both?

Address: 1–5 Wheat Road, Sydney 2000 (right next to Madame
Tussauds in Darling Harbour)

Website: **www.sydneyaquarium.com.au**

How to get there:  So easy! Walk down the hill from the city or
catch a train to Circular Quay then catch the ferry to Barangaroo
Wharf.  From there it's a short walk.

Opening hours: 10.00 am to 6.00 pm seven days.

Time budget:  At least two hours.

How much? Prices vary, but the best value deals if you book online include general admission plus the glass-bottom boat at around $60 for adults and $50 for children.  Other add-ons include the free Penguin Expedition boat ride or snuggle up to the penguins with a Penguin Passport for $199 per person.  For the truly adventurous there is the Shark Dive Xtreme for $299 per person.  Also consider the **Four Attractions Pass** (page 41).

While you're in the area:  Visit **Madame Tussauds** (page 42), the **WILD LIFE Sydney Zoo** (page 55) or visit the rest of **Darling Harbour** (page 40).

# The Sydney Tower Eye

Why you should go:  Because it truly offers the best and most panoramic view of the city of Sydney, 250 meters up (820 feet), short of taking a much more expensive helicopter ride.

Address: 100 Market Street, Sydney 2000

Website: **www.sydneytowereye.com.au**

How to get there:  Look up! It's right in the heart of the city and you can't miss it.  If coming from Central, catch the train to St James Station, then it's a short walk west down Market Street.

Opening hours: 9.00 am to last entry 8.00 pm seven days.

Time budget:  At least one hour.

How much? Tickets start at $23.20, because prices depend on when you visit, but also seriously consider the **Four Attractions Pass** (page 41).  For a truly spectacular experience see the New Year's Eve fireworks for $100 for adults and $65 for kids.  Alternatively, you might want to book a buffet or a dinner at the **360 Restaurant** (page 142).

While you're in the area: You're right in the heart of the city, so just take a look around and try finding the places that you spotted when you were high in the sky.  This is the heart of the city shopping precinct and you'll find all the major international and local brands around the pedestrian **Pitt Street Mall**, and in the Westfield shopping center and the Myer and David Jones department stores.

48 Darling Harbour as seen from Sydney Tower Eye

# Luna Park

Why you should go: Because Luna Park is one of Sydney's heritage-listed icons and an opportunity to experience a traditional fairground atmosphere. Few fairgrounds in the world offer a roller-coaster type ride and a Ferris wheel with harbor views.

Address: 1 Olympic Drive, Milsons Point 2016

Phone: 02 9922 6644

Website: **www.lunaparksydney.com**

How to get there: So easy! Catch a train to Circular Quay then catch the ferry to Milsons Point wharf, which is wheelchair accessible. From there it's a short walk. Alternatively, catch a train across the Sydney Harbour Bridge to Milsons Point Station.

Opening hours: Vary throughout the year but Luna Park is generally open Friday to Monday, with extended hours during school holidays. Best to check online or phone first.

Time budget: Three hours or more.

How much? Day tickets are, unusually, priced based on your height, rather than your age. Red Pass 85–105 cm $23, Green Pass 106–129 cm $43 and Yellow Pass 130 cm+ $53. Other group deals are available and you can save a little if you book online. Red and Green Pass holders require a paying adult to accompany them.

While you're in the area: If you're visiting during hot weather, you can pop into **North Sydney Olympic Pool**, which is right next door, either before or after Luna Park. Budget about $8.30 for adults, $4.20 for kids and a little more if you also want a spa or sauna. Open 5.30 am to 9.00 pm Monday to Friday and 7.00 am to 7.00 pm on the weekends. Phone: 02 9955 2309. If you want a fine dining experience, go to **Aqua Dining** (page 138) just above the pool.

# Taronga Zoo

Why you should go:  Because few places in the world offer not only the opportunity to see animals from all over the world but at the same time stunning harbor views.

Address:  Bradley's Head Road, Mosman 2000

Phone: 02 9969 2777

Website: **www.taronga.org.au**

How to get there:  Catch a train to Circular Quay then catch the ferry to Taronga Zoo Wharf.  Services depart every 30 minutes and the ride itself only takes 12 minutes.  If ferries make you seasick (although it's generally a very calm trip across the harbor), the M30 bus from either Central, Town Hall or Wynyard stations also leaves at 10-to-15-minute intervals.

Opening hours: 9.00 am to 4.30 pm seven days.

Time budget:  At least three hours but realistically it's an all-day trip.

How much? Tickets start at adults $42.30 (over 16), children $24.30 (4–15 years old) and under 4s are free.  For a truly unique glamping experience you can stay overnight at Taronga and have special extras with the Roar and Snore Experience.  Prices vary depending on when you go but start at $848.00 for a family of 2 adults and 2 children.  Check the website for more details.

While you're in the area: Over the warmer months top musical acts perform in the evening against the stunning backdrop of the harbor as part of the Twilight at Taronga series.  Go to **www.twilightattaronga.org.au** for more information and to check the lineup.  You can take a scenic walk through the bush along the harbor foreshore or stroll through the lovely suburb of Mosman, if you have any energy left.  There's just so much to Taronga Zoo you deserve an endurance medal if you have the energy and time for anything else.

# Virtual Reality Rooms

Why you should go: It might seem ironic that in an age when kids spend so much time on the computer you'd splurge to spend even more time in an electronic reality. But with several scenarios to choose from including 'Cosmos' and 'Mind Horror' this experience is designed to be truly immersive and is great fun, especially on a rainy day.

Address: Level 1, 484 Kent Street, Sydney 2000

Phone: 02 9267 3873

Website: **www.virtualrealityrooms.com.au**

How to get there: It's a five-minute walk from Town Hall Station

Opening hours: 9.00 am to 9.30 pm seven days.

Time budget: 90 minutes.

How much? $49 per person (Monday to Thursday) $59 per person (Friday to Sunday). Bookings essential.

While you're in the area: Head down to **Darling Harbour** (page 40), **Chinatown** (page 92) or browse the many boutique shops in the beautifully restored **Queen Victoria Building** (page 68).

## WILD LIFE Sydney Zoo

Why you should go:  Because if you don't have the stamina for Taronga, or if you have very young children, or if you don't want to spend the day just looking at animals, this is a better option and focuses on native wildlife.  Feeds and talks take place throughout the day.

Address: 1–5 Wheat Road, Sydney 2000

Website: **www.wildlifesydney.com.au**

How to get there:  So easy! It's a short walk west down King or Market streets from the CBD, or catch a train to Circular Quay then catch the ferry to Barangaroo Wharf.  From there it's a short walk south.

Opening hours: 10.00 am to 5.00 pm (last entry 4.00 pm) seven days.

Time budget: 90 minutes.

How much? Adults $44 and children $31 (online special) but also seriously consider the **Four Attractions Pass** (page 41).  Up to four people can have a photo taken with a koala for $25.

While you're in the area: **Madame Tussauds** (page 42) and **SEA LIFE Sydney Aquarium** (page 44) are just next door.  Then there's the rest of **Darling Harbour** (page 40) as well as **Barangaroo Reserve** (page 31) not too far away either.

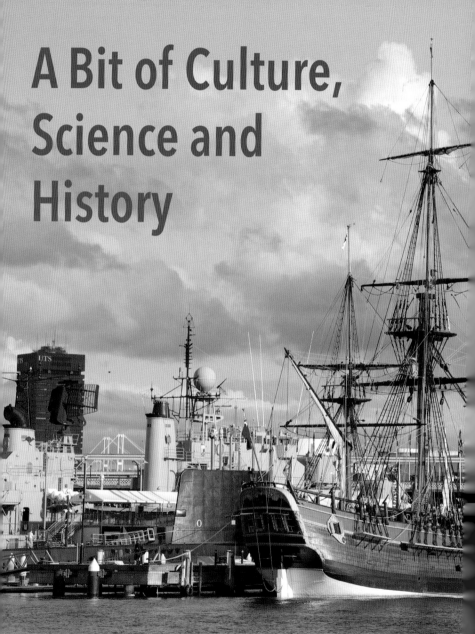

# A Bit of Culture, Science and History

Australian National Maritime Museum, Darling Harbour

For those of us whose idea of a holiday is cramming our brains with ever more information, or whose tastes run in the direction of science and history, here are a few must-see options when visiting Sydney.

## Anzac Memorial

Why you should go:  It commemorates the landing of Australian and New Zealand troops at Gallipoli in Turkey in World War I and the service and sacrifice of Australians in other armed conflicts.  Visiting the memorial is an extremely moving experience.

Address:  Hyde Park south (in the heart of the CBD, close to Liverpool Street)

Phone: 02 8262 2900

Website: **www.anzacmemorial.nsw.gov.au**

How to get there:  Walk from the city or catch a train to Museum Station then walk into Hyde Park.

Opening hours: 9.00 am to 5.00 pm seven days.

Time budget:  One hour.

How much? FREE!

While you're in the area: You're right in the heart of the city, so the choice is yours.  The nearby bus stop on Liverpool Street is also your departure point for buses to **Centennial Park** (page 38) and **Bondi Beach** (page 104).

# Australian National Maritime Museum

Why you should go:  Because if you're fascinated by ships and all things nautical, this is one of the best places to indulge that fascination in Sydney.

Address: 2 Murray Street, Sydney 2000

Phone: 02 9298 3777

Website: **www.anmm.gov.au**

How to get there:  It's a 15-minute walk from the CBD or from Central Station take the Light Rail which stops just across the road from the museum.

Opening hours: 9.30 am to 5.00 pm seven days.

Time budget:  Two to three hours.

How much? General admission to the permanent galleries is FREE! but the museum's Big Ticket deal gives you access to: special exhibitions, the Action Stations immersive experience, the 3D cinema, boarding access to the museum's vessels including the submarine, destroyer and tall ships, Kids on Deck activities and daily guided tours.  Adults $32, concessions and children (4–15) $20, children under 4, free.

While you're in the area: You're at the western end of **Darling Harbour** (page 40), so you can walk across **Pyrmont Bridge** to visit the attractions on the other side.  Go for a five-minute walk west of the museum to visit **Star Casino** with its range of restaurants and the **Lyric Theatre**.

# Chinese Garden of Friendship

Why you should go:  Because it was a gift from the Chinese government to Australia, designed in Sydney's Chinese sister city of Guangzhou.  Gardening enthusiasts will adore it.  It's also an island of calm and peace – a great place to recharge your spiritual batteries.

Address:  Corner of Pier Street and Harbour Street, Darling Harbour 2000

Website: **www.darlingharbour.com/things-to-do/ chinese-garden-of-friendship**

How to get there:  It's a 10-minute stroll north-west from Central Station through Chinatown.  Much longer than 10 minutes if you're tempted to linger and wander in **Chinatown** (page 91).

Opening hours: 9.30 am to 5.00 pm seven days from April to September and till 5.30 pm from October to March.

Time budget:  At least one hour.

How much? Adults $6, concessions and children under 12 $3, families (2 adults and 2 children) $15.  There's also the onsite restaurant **Gardens by Lotus**, open for lunch from 11.00 am to 3.00 pm seven days and for dinner 6.00 pm to 8.30 pm Wednesday to Sunday;  Phone: 02 8311 5156.

While you're in the area: You're at the southern end of **Darling Harbour** (page 40), so you can go north and visit the rest of it, or south-west will take you to the **Powerhouse Museum** (page 78) or directly south is **Chinatown** and **Paddy's Market** (page 91).  If you're hungry, just south is the **Golden Century Seafood Restaurant** (page 140).

ntemporary
Art

Museum of
Contemporary
Art Australia

## Museum of Contemporary Art

Why you should go: For the spectacular waterfront location between The Rocks and Circular Quay and because it's an excellent first stop if you want to know more about the contemporary art scene in Sydney.

Address: 140 George Street, The Rocks 2000

Phone: 02 9245 2400

Website: **www.mca.com.au**

How to get there: It's a 10-minute slow stroll north-west from Circular Quay Station. It's a big, heritage-listed sandstone, concrete and glass building facing the water. You can't miss it.

Opening hours: 10.00 am to 5.00 pm daily and open till 9.00 pm Wednesdays.

Time budget: At least an hour.

How much? FREE! But there are charges for special exhibitions. These usually hover around the $20 mark for general admission.

While you're in the area: You're at the southern end of **The Rocks** (page 26), or walk around **Circular Quay** to the **Sydney Opera House** (page 24), and then on to the **Royal Botanic Gardens** (page 33).

# State Library of New South Wales

Why you should go:  Because it's a must if you're a bibliophile, especially if you want to look at some of the significant special collections, and it's a nice place to spend some time if you're in the vicinity of the **Royal Botanic Gardens** (page 33) and you've already visited the **Art Gallery of NSW** (page 29).

Address:  Macquarie Street, Sydney 2000 (near the corner of Hunter Street)

Phone: 02 9273 1414

Website: **www.sl.nsw.gov.au**

How to get there:  Take the train to Martin Place Station. Walk uphill until you reach Macquarie Street at the top. Cross the road, turn left.  You're there in five minutes.

Opening hours: 9.00 am to 8.00 pm Saturday to Thursday, 9.00 am to 5.00 pm Friday.  Different parts of the library, like exhibition rooms, open at different times.  Phone ahead or visit the website to plan your visit.

Time budget:  At least an hour.

How much? FREE! Library tours are free too and special exhibitions are almost always free.  Like everywhere else that's free, they appreciate donations – that good karma thing again.

While you're in the area: Macquarie Street is a sort of 'Museum Road' with a special group of attractions called **Sydney Living Museums** (page 70).

## Queen Victoria Building

Why you should go:  Because it's an excellent example of the restoration and repurposing of a heritage-listed building, built in the late 1880s as a marketplace. It's a bit of a feast for a shopper too. Don't miss the grand central dome, stained-glass windows and mechanical clocks.

Address:  455 George Street, Sydney 2000 (next to Town Hall)
Phone: 02 9265 6800

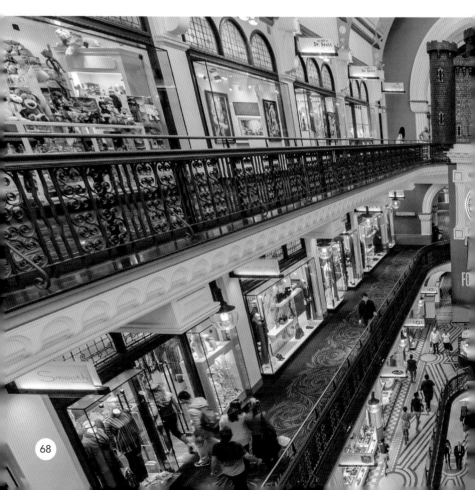

Website: **www.qvb.com.au**

How to get there: Take the train to Town Hall Station. Leave via the northern exit and veer left and you'll find yourself in its lower levels.

Opening hours: 9.00 am to 6.00 pm Monday to Saturday, 9.00 am to 9.00 pm Thursday, 11am to 5pm Sunday.

While you're in the area: Browse the nearby majestic Victorian-era **Strand Arcade** (412–414 George Street, Sydney; Website: **www.strandarcade.com.au**) or walk down Market Street to **Darling Harbour** (page 40).

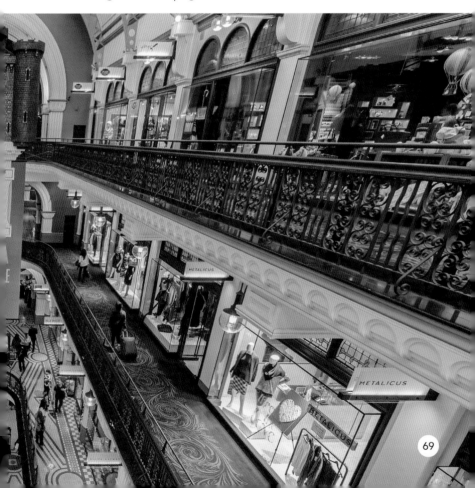

## Sydney Living Museums –
## Macquarie Street and nearby

What were once a group of separate small museums in Sydney have now come under one collective vision. All are dedicated to giving visitors a greater insight into Sydney's history. Opening hours vary so phone or go to the website to plan your visit to Sydney's own memory lane, all a short walk from Martin Place Station.

Website: **www.sydneylivingmuseums.com.au**

## Hyde Park Barracks Museum

Dedicated to the history of convicts.

Address: Queens Square, Macquarie Street, Sydney 2000
   (near the corner of College Street); Phone: 02 8239 2288
Admission: FREE!

## The Mint

Dedicated to the history of money. The Mint is also the home of the Caroline Simpson Library and Research Collection and is dedicated to the history of house and garden design and interior furnishing in New South Wales, so you can see how the settlers of New South Wales spent some of their money too.

Address: 10 Macquarie Street, Sydney 2000;
  Phone: 02 8239 2288
Admission: FREE!

## Reserve Bank of Australia Museum

Dedicated to the history of even more money. Not part of the Living Museums group, but it's close to all the others, so you might as well take a peak.

Address: 65 Martin Place, Sydney 2000; Phone: 02 9551 9743
Admission: FREE!

## Museum of Sydney

Dedicated to the early years of Sydney's foundation and establishment and located on the site of the first Government House.

Address:  Corner of Bridge Street and Phillip Street, Sydney 2000; Phone: 02 9251 5988

Admission:  Adults $15, concessions $12, family (2 adults, 2 children) $38, children 4 and under free.

## Justice & Police Museum

Dedicated to the early years of crime and punishment.

Address:  Corner of Albert Street and Elizabeth Street, Circular Quay 2000;  Phone: 02 9252 1144

Admission:  Adults $12, concessions $8, family (2 adults, 2 children or 1 adult, 3 children) $30, children 4 and under free.

## SPECIAL MUSEUM AND HISTORIC HOUSES DEAL

Purchase a **Sydney Museums Pass** online or from any of the participating museums and historic houses listed below and get access to all the attractions for one month from the date of your first visit to any of the sites – one visit per venue.

How much? Adults $24, concessions and children (ages 5 to 15) $16, family (2 adults, 2 children or 1 adult, 3 children) $50, children 4 and under free.

Website: **www.sydneylivingmuseums.com.au/sydney-museums-pass** or visit any of the participating venues and buy the pass on site.

## Participating Museums and Historic Houses

- Elizabeth Bay House
- Elizabeth Farm
- Hyde Park Barracks Museum
- Justice and Police Museum
- Meroogal
- Museum of Sydney
- Rose Seidler House
- Rouse Hill House and Farm
- Susannah Place Museum
- The Caroline Simpson Library and Research Collection
- The Mint
- Vaucluse House

# St Mary's Cathedral

Why you should go:  Sydney doesn't have the long history of spectacular cathedral building that Europe has, but St Mary's is a pretty good attempt at emulating the tradition, and is still a beautiful building and a haven of peace in the inner city.

Address:  College Street, Sydney 2000 (opposite the northern end of Hyde Park)

Phone: 02 9220 0400

Website: **www.stmaryscathedral.org.au**

How to get there: It's a pleasant five-minute walk east across Hyde Park.  The closest railway station is St James.

Opening hours: 6.30 am to about 6.00 pm seven days

Time budget:  At least one hour, especially if you plan to attend mass.

How much? FREE! But donations are always welcome.  There are also free tours every Sunday at 10.30 am after the morning mass.

While you're in the area: Visit some of the **Sydney Living Museums** along Macquarie Street and nearby (page 70).  Take a stroll through **Hyde Park** or go into the city.  **The Australian Museum** (page 76) is just across William Street too.

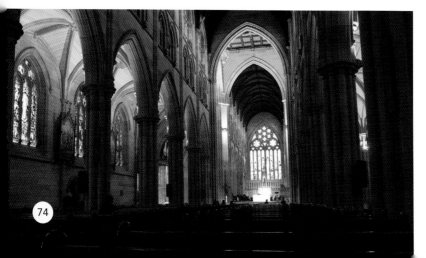

# Australian Museum

Why you should go: Because it's the biggest museum in New South Wales that is dedicated to natural history.

Address: 1 William Street, Sydney 2000 (opposite the south-eastern end of Hyde Park)

Phone: 02 9320 6000

Website: **www.australianmuseum.net.au**

How to get there: It's a short walk from the CBD, or take the train to Museum Station then cut across Hyde Park, or walk up Liverpool Street then turn left onto College Street. The museum is on the corner of College Street and William Street.

Opening hours: 9.30 am to 5.00 pm seven days.

Time budget: At least three hours, there's a lot to see.

How much? Adults $15, concessions $8, children 15 and under free but must be accompanied by a supervising adult. All tickets entitle holders to unlimited entry on the day of purchase, so don't lose your ticket if you plan to come back on the day! Special exhibitions are extra. Free audio tours are also available.

While you're in the area: Visit some of the **Sydney Living Museums** (page 70) along Macquarie Street and nearby to the north. Take a stroll through Hyde Park or go into the city. **St Mary's Cathedral** (page 74), **The Anzac Memorial** (page 59) and the **Australian Museum of Magical Arts** (page 86) are nearby too.

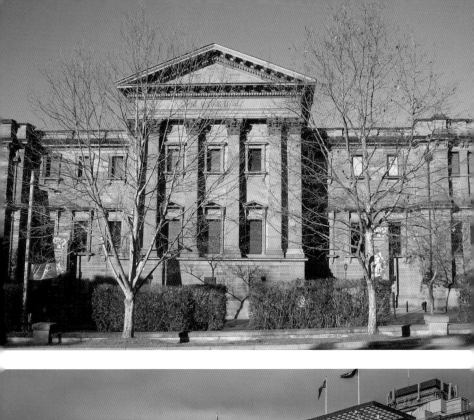

## Powerhouse Museum

Why you should go:  Because it's the biggest museum in
New South Wales dedicated to science and technology.
Now officially known as part of the **Museum of Applied Arts
and Sciences**, its collection comprises more than 400,000
objects.

Address: 500 Harris Street, Ultimo 2000

Phone: 02 9217 0111

Website: **www.maas.museum/powerhouse-museum**

How to get there:  Catch the Light Rail from Central and get off at
the Ian Thorpe Aquatic Centre. From there it's a short walk south.

Opening hours: 10.00 am to 5.00 pm seven days.

Time budget: At least three hours, there's a lot to see.

How much? Adults $15, concessions $8, children 16 and under free. Free general admission for teachers. All tickets entitle holders to unlimited entry on the day of purchase, so don't lose your ticket if you plan to come back on the same day! Special exhibitions are extra.

While you're in the area: Take a stroll through **Chinatown** and **Paddy's Market** (page 91) and the **Chinese Garden of Friendship** (page 63).

# Sydney Harbour Tall Ships

Why you should go:  Sydney Harbour Tall Ships offer a variety of harbor cruises on traditional sailing vessels.  There aren't too many places in the world where you can do this – and in such a lovely setting too.

Address:  Wharf 5, Circular Quay 2000

Phone: 02 8015 5571

Website: **www.sydneytallships.com.au**

How to get there:  Catch the train to Circular Quay, the wharves are just outside the station.

Opening hours:  Vary depending on cruise.

Time budget:  At least two hours.

How much? Prices vary depending on the cruise and the time of year and start at around $99 for adults and $49 for children for lunch cruises.  For a fun time with the kids, checkout the **Pineapple Pirates' cruise** (page 43).  Bookings essential.  Cruises leave from various points around Sydney Harbour, but they'll give you a map when you book.

While you're in the area: Take a stroll through **The Rocks** (page 26) or visit the **Museum of Contemporary Art** (page 65).

# Sydney Observatory

Why you should go:  Because if you want to indulge your inner astronomer, this is the place to go.  You also get spectacular views across the harbor from its location at the top of Observatory Hill.

Address: 1003 Upper Fort Street, Millers Point 2000

Phone: 02 9217 0111

Website: **www.maas.museum/sydney-observatory**

How to get there:  Catch the train to Circular Quay.  From there head west up Argyle Street through The Rocks before turning left onto Watson Street, which becomes Upper Fort Street.  It's a 15-minute walk, but it's almost all uphill.  It is an observatory after all. Alternatively, you can catch the train to Wynyard Station and walk north along York Street and then Kent Street.  It's slightly less strenuous.  It's best to look at a map, because either way is a bit tricky.

Opening hours: 10.00 am to 5.00 pm seven days for day visits.  Night visits vary according to the time of year.

Time budget:  At least two hours, especially if you plan to visit the planetarium

How much? Day tours:  Adults $10, concessions and children (4–16) $8, free for children 3 and under, families $26.00 (2 adults, 2 children or 1 adult, 3 children).  Night tours:  Adults $27, concessions $25, children (4–16) $20, free for children 3 and under, families $80 (2 adults, 2 children or 1 adult, 3 children).  All children must be accompanied by an adult.  Bookings essential.  You can also have a permanent reminder of your Sydney visit by naming a star: **www.maas.museum/sydney-observatory/name-a-star**

While you're in the area: Take a stroll downhill to **The Rocks** (page 26) or take advantage of the fact that you're already high up and take a walk along the **Sydney Harbour Bridge** (page 22). Or if you just want to sit down and have a pub meal after all that stargazing the **Hero of Waterloo** (page 145) and the **Harbour View Hotel** (page 145) are just a stone's throw away – both in Lower Fort Street.

# Off the Beaten Tourist Track and Nice if You Have the Time

University of Sydney

# Australian Museum of Magical Arts

An immersive experience for fans of magic hidden within the **Magicians Cabaret Theatre**, which houses weekly magic shows. The museum of magic consists of a library of magic and a collection of magical paraphernalia and illusions. You are led by the magician and will experience first-hand how a magician orchestrates their magic show.

Address: 91 Riley Street, Darlinghurst 2010

Phone: 02 9267 4747

Website: **www.sydneymuseums.com.au**

Opening hours: Admission by day tour, guided by a magician, bookings essential. Tuesday to Friday 11.30 am and 1.30 pm, Saturday and Sunday 1.30 pm.

How much? Adults $41, concessions and children under 12 accompanied by an adult $31. A dusk tour is also available on Tuesdays and Wednesdays at 7 pm for $55 per person.

Time budget: One hour.

While you're in the area: Head back up the hill to **The Australian Museum** (page 76), which is just a five-minute walk west or continue on to **Hyde Park** and the **Anzac Memorial** (page 59).

# Brett Whiteley Studio

Why you should go:  This extension of the Art Gallery of New South Wales preserves the workplace and home of one of Australia's most well-known modern artists and gives you a real insight into the working life and creative process of an artist.

Address: 2 Raper Street, Surry Hills 2010

Phone: 02 9225 1881

Website: **www.artgallery.nsw.gov.au/brett-whiteley-studio**

How to get there:  The new Sydney South East Light Rail is due to open at the end of 2019 and it will be a short walk from Devonshire Street. Otherwise, check the transport Trip Planner for buses or it's a 15-minute walk from Central Station.  Go east along Foveaux Street until you hit Crown Street.  Go south along Crown Street until you see Davies Street on your left (the fourth street).  From there walk until you reach Raper Street.

Opening hours: 10.00 am to 4.00 pm Friday to Sunday.

Time budget:  One to two hours.

How much:  FREE!

While you're in the area: Surry Hills is a center of Sydney's cafe culture and home to many highly regarded bars and restaurants. You can also browse the small, eclectic shops.  If you happen to be visiting on the first Saturday of the month be sure to check out **Surry Hills markets** at the park between Foveaux Street and Collins Street, opposite the library, for a range of handcrafts, vintage clothing and antiques.

# Carriageworks

Why you should go: Another great example of the creative reuse of an industrial site, the massive sheds were built in the late 1880s as part of the Eveleigh Railway Workshops. In 2007 the disused site was redeveloped as a cultural precinct and it now hosts a wide range of arts performances and a much-loved Saturday farmers' market.

Address: 245 Wilson Street, Eveleigh 2015

Phone: 02 8571 9099

Website: **www.carriageworks.com.au**

How to get there: Take the train from Central Station and get off at Redfern. Carriageworks is about 10 minutes' walk south-west. Bus routes 422, 423, 426, 428, 370 and 352 stop on City Road at Butlin Avenue, which turns into Codrington Street – Carriageworks is a 10-minute walk south.

Opening hours: 10.00 am to 6.00 pm seven days; farmers' market Saturdays from 8.00 am to 1.00 pm.

Time budget: Two to three hours including travel time.

How much: Free to look around. Costs vary for special exhibitions and concerts so check the website to see what's on.

While you're in the area: Wander back through Chippendale and check out the **White Rabbit Gallery** (30 Balfour Street, Chippendale), a free modern-art gallery showcasing contemporary Chinese art and with its own Chinese teahouse. If you're hungry, continue on to **Kensington St and Spice Alley** (page 143).

WITHIN THE FOUR SEAS ALL MEN ARE BROTHERS

四海一家

# Chinatown and Paddy's Market

Not exactly 'off the beaten track' but not exactly on it either, Chinatown and Paddy's Market are adjacent precincts just west of Central Station and are fine places to just stroll and have a look around. If you prefer, just take the Light Rail from Central and get off at the Paddy's Market stop.

There are plenty of places to eat and so many shops and stalls that you're likely to find all sorts of things that you won't find anywhere else. Besides shopping it's a nice idea to try yum cha one morning for brunch at any number of different places in the precinct.

Website: **www.paddysmarkets.com.au**

Opening hours: Chinatown is open all the time with many restaurants open until the early hours; Paddy's Market is open Wednesday to Sunday from 10.00 am to 6.00 pm.

Time budget: About two hours.

While you're in the area: You're not far from the **Powerhouse Museum** (page 78), the **Chinese Garden of Friendship** (page 63) and **Darling Harbour** (page 40).

## Culture Scouts Walking Tours

For the art buffs Culture Scouts offer some offbeat tours in some of Sydney's even more offbeat suburbs.  Fun to do if your tastes run to urban landscapes, street art, galleries and inner-city culture.

Tours include Chippendale Art Month, Darlinghurst and Surry Hills, Discover Ultimo and Chinatown, Inner West, Surry Hills Art Month, Sydney Street Art and many others.  Contact them and tell them what you're interested in and see what's available.

Phone: 1300 776 043

Website: **www.culturescouts.com.au**

How much? From $50 per person.

Time budget:  At least two hours.

Paddington Reservoir Gardens

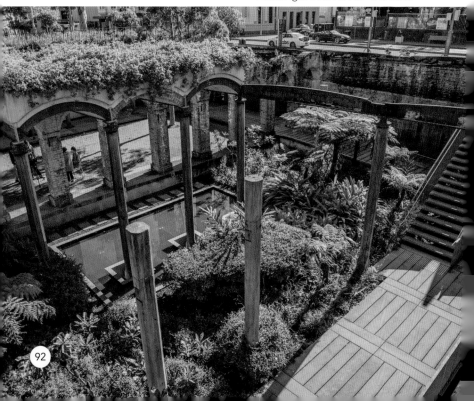

## The Sydney Connection

The Sydney Connection organizes dining walks for small groups around the interesting inner-city suburbs of Potts Point, Darlinghurst and Surry Hills. The foodie tours are a great way to meet like-minded travelers, visit some of Sydney's most loved bars and restaurants and go where the locals go. Guests visit four different venues, sampling a dish with a matched glass of wine at each.

Phone: 0435 050 367

Website: **www.thesydneyconnection.com.au**

How much? $165 per person for three course, $195 per person for four courses. Special tours can be arranged for families with children.

# Nicholson Museum at the University of Sydney

Why you should go: Because it's one of Sydney's lesser-known museums so you won't be fighting off the crowds. Founded in 1860 it houses a collection of some 30,000 artifacts from all over the world. The museum is on the grounds of the University of Sydney, which is in itself an interesting place to visit and a nice place to spend some quiet time.

Address: Manning Road, Camperdown 2050

Phone: 02 9351 2812

Website: **www.sydney.edu.au/museums/collections/nicholson**

How to get there: A five-minute walk just west of Central Station will take you to the **Railway Square** Bus Interchange. There's an information booth there or just ask a bus driver. Take any bus headed up Parramatta Road – Routes 412, 413, 436, 438, 439, 440, 461, 480, 483 or Metrobus M10 – and alight at the Footbridge stop. If in doubt, ask the bus driver to let you know when to get off. From there it's a five-minute walk south. Google Maps will be your best friend here. The museum is at the southern entrance of the Quadrangle at the University of Sydney.

Opening hours: 10.00 am to 4.30 pm Monday to Friday, also open on the first Saturday of every month 12 pm to 4 pm.

Time budget: About two hours including travel time.

How much: FREE! Donations welcome.

While you're in the area: Wander east to Victoria Park. Veer north back to Parramatta Road Broadway but keep walking east. After a 10-minute walk you will get to **Kensington Street and Spice Alley** (page 143) where you'll need to prepare yourself for the huge range of eateries and shopperies that you will encounter there.

# Sydney Fish Market

Why you should go:  Sydneysiders love their seafood, and with a wide range of top-quality produce, even chefs come to the fish market to select the catch of the day.  On Christmas Eve thousands flock to the markets to stock up on prawns and other delicacies for their Christmas feast and the market trades continuously for 36 hours.  If you're a fan of seafood, or if you just love the market atmosphere in general, the Sydney Fish Market is a nice place to visit and have lunch.

Address:  Corner of Pyrmont Bridge Road and Bank Street, Pyrmont 2009

Phone: 02 9004 1100

Website: **www.sydneyfishmarket.com.au**

How to get there:  Easy! Catch the Light Rail from Central and get off at the Fish Market stop.

Opening hours:  The wholesale auction takes place at 5.30 am weekdays.  Retailers generally open from 7.00 am and close around 4.00 pm on weekdays with some open until 5.00 pm Friday to Sunday.  **Fisherman's Wharf** restaurant is open for dinner until 11.00 pm every night.

Time budget:  About an hour and longer if you plan to eat.

How much:  If you're super-keen you can go on a behind-the-scenes tour, held every weekday at 6.40 am.  Bookings essential.  Phone 02 9004 1108 or visit **www.sydneyfishmarket.com.au/at-the-market/tours**.  Adults $45, children (10–13) $20.  For safety reasons the minimum age of tour participants is 10.  All participants *must* wear enclosed shoes.  Avoid wearing leather shoes as they tend to absorb fishy-smelling water.

# Sydney Jewish Museum

Why you should go:  Because you don't have to be Jewish to be interested in the history of one of the most prominent ethnic groups to have settled in Australia.  The museum is a serious place for the serious minded but it's also fascinating, moving and very educational.

Address: 148 Darlinghurst Road, Darlinghurst, on the corner of Darlinghurst Road and Burton Street

Phone: 02 9360 7999

Website: **www.sydneyjewishmuseum.com.au**

How to get there:  Catch the train to Kings Cross Station and walk south along Darlinghurst Road for about 10 minutes.  Alternatively, take a bus from the city up Oxford Street, get off at Taylor Square and walk north along Darlinghurst Road.

Opening hours: 10.00 am to 4.30 pm Monday to Thursday, 10.00 am to 3.30 pm Friday, 10.00 am to 4.00 pm Sunday.  Closed Saturdays and on some Jewish holidays.

Time budget:  About 1½ hours to 2 hours.

How much:  Adults $15, seniors $12, children $9, children under 10 free, family (2 adults and 2 children) $40.

While you're in the area: Darlinghurst has traditionally been the heart of Sydney's gay and lesbian community and a hub for bohemian writers, musicians and artists.  There are many interesting cafes, restaurants and bars around Darlinghurst, Kings Cross and Potts Point so you might like to wander the streets and explore.  You can catch a train back to the city from Kings Cross Station.  Alternatively, keep walking south along Darlinghurst Road until you hit Oxford Street.  From there you can catch buses either heading west back to the city or east to **Centennial Park** (page 38) or further on to Bondi Junction and **Bondi Beach** (page 104).

## Tramsheds

Why you should go:  The former Rozelle Tramway Depot (built in 1904) hosts a plethora of places to eat and shop and is a great example of what to do when you have an old industrial site and you want to spruce it up for the tastes of gentrified city dwellers.

Address: 1 Dalgal Way, Forest Lodge

Phone: 02 8398 5695

Website: **www.tramshedssydney.com.au**

How to get there:  Take the Light Rail from Central Station and get off at Jubilee Park.  From there it's a two-minute stroll.

Opening hours: 7.00 am to 10.00 pm seven days.

Time budget:  About two hours.

How much:  FREE! Spend as much as you want on food and other shopping.

While you're in the area:  If the weather is good, take a stroll through **Jubilee Park** and the **Glebe Foreshore** parks.  Hug the shoreline and you'll see the **Sydney Superyacht Marina**.  If you are visiting on a Saturday, walk up Glebe Point Road and visit the **Glebe Markets** (page 114).

## The Grounds of Alexandria

Why you should go: What do you get when you create a combination cafe, bakery, eatery and organic gardens around a courtyard in a converted industrial pie factory? It's kid-friendly, dog-friendly and Instagram-friendly with a menagerie that includes the latest addition, a pig called Harry Trotter.

Address: 7a/2 Huntley St, Alexandria 2015

Phone: 02 9699 2225

Website: **www.thegrounds.com.au**

How to get there:  Take the train to Green Square Station and take the Bourke Road exit. Walk south on Bourke Road for about 10 minutes until you get to Huntley Street and it's right on the corner.

Opening hours: 7.00 am to
9.00 pm Monday to Thursday,
7.00 am to 10 pm Friday,
7.30 am to 10 pm Saturday;
7.30 am to 9 pm Sunday.

Time budget: About two hours

While you're in the area:
The Grounds is in a light
industrial area and there's
not much else around unless
you're renovating your house
or need to get your car
repaired. If you're visiting
with kids they might like to
burn off some energy at:

**Skyzone** indoor trampoline
park and climbing center,
about a 5-minte walk
south-east (75 O'Riordan
Street, Alexandria, 2015;
Phone: 137599; Website:
**www.skyzone.com.au/
locations/alexandria**).

If the kids prefer ice skating
to jumping **Ice Zoo Sydney**
is about a 10-minute walk
south of The Grounds (689
Gardeners Road, Alexandria,
2015; Phone: 02 9669 6445;
Website: **www.icezoo.com**).

# The Great Outdoors

Not all of Sydney's attractions lie within roofed walls. Sydney is full of natural landscapes that are the envy of many of the world's cities. Sydney's beaches are justly famous and since many of them link to each other you can incorporate your beach visits into a larger plan to get in some walking. Your go-to sites for these walks

Bondi Beach

are **www.sydneycoastwalks.com.au** and **www.bestsydneywalks.com/sydney-harbour-national-park-walks**.

Sydney has a lot of land devoted to green areas that are pretty obvious if you look at any map, and that are worth visiting if you've had enough of the city and are craving some nature. If you like bushwalking you could head to **Ku-ring-gai Chase National Park** in the north or **Royal National Park** in the south, one of the oldest national parks in the world. The most accessible parklands from the CBD are the **Royal Botanic Gardens** (page 33) and **Centennial Park** (page 38).

## Bondi Beach

Arguably the most famous beach in Australia, and certainly one of the most visited tourist destinations.  There are not too many cities in the world where you can leave work and be at such a stunning beach in under an hour – it's just 10 kilometres (6 miles) from the CBD.

How to get there:  From Central Station catch the train on the Eastern Suburbs line to Bondi Junction.  From the Bondi Junction interchange, catch the 380, 381, 382 or 333 bus to Bondi Beach.  The total trip takes about 45 minutes.  In summer the buses can be VERY busy. You have been warned.

While you're there:  Bondi Beach is home to some of Sydney's best restaurants, bars and shops (see **Icebergs** page 136) and many lovely Art Deco buildings.  From Bondi Beach you can take the **Bondi to Coogee Beach coastal walk**.  Just hug the coast and keep going.  Remember to take sunscreen, water and a jacket in case it gets windy and cold.  Walk length about 6.5 kilometres (about 4 miles). Coogee Beach is smaller and much less crowded.

## Manly Beach

Another famous large beach, less visited than Bondi because the trip from the CBD is longer (but frankly, much more pleasant), but once you're there, there's plenty to see and do in **Manly** (page 34).

How to get there:  From Central Station catch the train to Circular Quay then catch the ferry to Manly.  Then it's a 10-minute stroll along the shop-and-restaurant-lined Corso to Manly Beach.  Budget about an hour for the whole trip if you're taking your time, longer if you miss the connections.

While you're there:  Even if you have no interest in shopping, eating or doing an activity, on a good weather day there's the great **Manly to the Spit walk** via Shelly Beach.  The walk is officially 10 kilometres (6.2 miles) so take plenty of water and the usual sun protection.  At a leisurely pace it will take you about five hours.  From Spit Bridge there are a number of buses that will take you back to the CBD.

## Maroubra Beach

This lesser-known beach is much loved by the locals because even though it has experienced some development, it's the closest thing to what beaches used to be like in Australia 50 years ago. A large sweeping beach, it's relatively close to the CBD while still being off the beaten tourist track.

How to get there: Catch the 376 bus from the Eddy Avenue bus stops at Central Station. The trip takes about 45 minutes.

While You're There: Eat at one of the many eateries in the area. There really isn't much else to do except just relax, so it's the perfect beach to go to when you only want a quiet day at the beach without having to go too far to avoid the crowds.

## Nielsen Park and The Hermitage Foreshore Walk

Nielsen Park is perfectly positioned on the harbour at Vaucluse in Sydney's eastern suburbs, just south of **Watsons Bay** (page 109). Shark Beach is a lovely place to swim, particularly for kids, with golden sand and much calmer water than the ocean beaches. The views across the harbor back to the city are sublime and there's a large, shady park with magnificent old fig trees, picnic areas and a cafe. If you're feeling more energetic the **Hermitage Foreshore walk** is an easy 1.8-kilometre walk along the harbor taking in Nielsen Park and the heritage-listed **Strickland House**.

How to get there: Vaucluse is on the 324 and 325 bus routes. To plan your trip go to **www.transportnsw.info**. You can catch the bus all the way from the city, or from Central Station catch the train on the Eastern Suburbs line to Edgecliff Station. From the Edgecliff bus interchange, above the station, catch a 324 or 325 bus.

While you're there: **Vaucluse House** (Wentworth Road, Vaucluse) is a nineteenth-century mansion that is part of the **Sydney Living Museums** (page 70) and is surrounded by its original gardens. You can also visit the tearooms for a traditional high tea (**www.vauclusehousetearooms.com.au**). Nearby, **Parsley Bay** is another lovely, calm harbor beach with a lush park for picnics and a playground for the kids.

## Palm Beach

Sydney's northernmost ocean beach, Palm Beach is at the end of a long peninsula with the surf of the Pacific Ocean on one side and the tranquil Pittwater on the other. Palm Beach is also famous as the location of the long-running TV soap opera *Home and Away*.

How to get there: It's about an hour's drive from the city or the L90 bus route leaves from Wynyard Station in the city and takes about 90 minutes. If you want to make it an experience you won't forget, you can travel in style on a 20-minute scenic seaplane flight from Rose Bay (**www.sydneybyseaplane.com**).

While you're there: Hike up to **Barrenjoey Lighthouse** for spectacular views across Pittwater and back down the coastline, enjoy a meal at one of the delicious cafes and restaurants or take the ferry across Pittwater to the fishing village of **Patonga**.

## Watsons Bay

Why you should go:  Because while it's still reasonably close to the CBD its far enough away to feel like a coastal getaway and not have that touristy feel.  It's also pretty.

How to get there:  The most picturesque way to travel is by ferry, leaving every hour from Wharf 6 at Circular Quay and stopping at Double Bay wharf and Rose Bay wharf on the way to Watsons Bay – travel time about an hour.  Otherwise, you can get there by bus. The 324 bus leaves from near Town Hall Station at Park Street, Stand G and will take you through Sydney's southern-harbor-hugging suburbs – travel time about an hour.

Time budget:  Three hours and up if you include travel time.

While you're there:  If you like seafood, eat at **Doyles** (page 136). If you're in the mood for brunch in a historic-house setting, go to **Dunbar House** (**www.dunbarhouse.com.au**).  If you like something more active there's snorkeling at **Camp Cove**. You can visit the Hornby Lighthouse and the nearby keeper's cottage. Watsons Bay is also home to Sydney's most famous nude beach, **Lady Bay**.  Not recommended in cold weather.

# Sydney Harbour National Park
# and Cockatoo Island

Even many Sydneysiders are unaware that a lot of land along Sydney Harbour foreshore and all the islands in the harbor are administered by an entity known as the Sydney Harbour National Park. The go-to site for more information is **www.nationalparks.nsw.gov.au/visit-a-park/parks/sydney-harbour-national-park**.

Getting access to the islands can be a bit tricky, as the park's authority reserves the right to close them for maintenance at unpredictable times, even if you have access to a boat or a kayak. Although Sydney Harbour is dotted with islands the most interesting to visit is:

## Cockatoo Island

Cockatoo Island is the largest and easily the most accessible of the islands and available year-round. Cockatoo Island was once a convict penal establishment, reformatory school and naval ship dockyard but it now regularly hosts major art events including the **Biennale of Sydney**. There are a number of accommodation options on the island including popular 'glamping' sites. Harbour City Ferries run regular services to Cockatoo Island. Website: **www.cockatooisland.gov.au/visit**.

# Markets

Wandering through local markets is a popular weekend pastime for locals, whether it's for fresh produce, vintage bargains or up-and-coming designers, with each market having a different focus. Markets are often located in some of the oldest and most interesting parts of the city so can be a great introduction to a neighborhood and its inhabitants. Here are a few to get you started (also see **The Rocks** (page 26), **Surry Hills** and its various attractions (page 87) and **Carriageworks** (page 88).

## Glebe

Weekly market held each Saturday from 10.00 am to 4.00 pm on the grounds of Glebe Public School, on Glebe Point Road, Glebe. Find vintage clothing, jewelry, accessories, food and live performers.

## Kings Cross

Kings Cross was the bohemian heart of Sydney and the markets reflect the diversity of the area. Held from 9.00 am to 2.00 pm on Saturdays and from 10 am to 3.00 pm on Sundays at Fitzroy Gardens, Macleay Street, Potts Point. Expect to find fresh and organic gourmet produce, fresh flowers and plants as well as antiques and local art.

## Paddington

Operating since 1973, Paddington Markets have launched the careers of some of Australia's most well known designers. Great for unique fashion and gifts, homewares, jewelry and accessories. Every Saturday, rain or shine, 10 am to 4.00 pm, 395–435 Oxford Street, Paddington (on the grounds of Paddington Public School and the Paddington Uniting Church), right near **Centennial Park** (page 38).

## Kirribilli

From 8.30 am till 3.00 pm on the second and fourth Sunday of the month, focusing on new and vintage fashion, art and design. Gorgeous location on the northern side of the Harbour Bridge, Burton Street, Milsons Point.

## Bondi Beach

Sundays from 10.00 am to 4.00 pm on the grounds of Bondi Beach Public School, Campbell Parade, Bondi Beach. Up-and-coming local designer clothing, jewelry, art and homewares.

# Beyond the City

The Three Sisters, Katoomba

Not all the delights of Sydney are located in the CBD. Getting out of the city center will let you see a different side of the multicultural metropolis that is Sydney.

## Parramatta

If you want to do something a little different you can head west to Parramatta, Sydney's *other* CBD. Located on the banks of the Parramatta River, Parramatta has been home to the Darug people for more than 60,000 years. The city of Parramatta was founded by British colonists the same year as the city of Sydney, 1788, and features many interesting sites from colonial times. It is now a major business and commercial center with shopping, dining and nightlife located around Church Street.

If you want to plan your trip ahead of time contact the **Parramatta Heritage and Visitor Information Centre**. The staff are very helpful and can suggest a number of things to see and do in the Parramatta area.
Address: 346a Church Street, Parramatta 2150
Phone: 02 8839 3311
Website: **www.discoverparramatta.com**
Opening hours: 9.00 am to 5.00 pm Monday to Friday, 10.00 am to 4.00 pm weekends and public holidays.
How to get there: From Central Station catch a train to Parramatta Station. From there it's a 10-minute stroll to Church Street, or the FREE 900 shuttle bus from Macquarie Street will take you on a 25-minute loop. The more scenic way to get to Parramatta is to catch the ferry from Circular Quay. Check before traveling as at the time of writing the Parramatta ferry wharf was closed for an upgrade until late 2019.

# Featherdale Wildlife Park

Why you should go:  Because it's a nice place for families and is home to almost 2000 reptiles, birds and mammals with a heavy emphasis on native wildlife.  It also has a picnic area and souvenir shop.

Address: 217 Kildare Road, Doonside 2767

Phone: 02 9622 1644

Website: **www.featherdale.com.au**

How to get there:  Unless you have a car, the easiest way to get to Featherdale is with one of the tour operators that include it on their schedule (check Featherdale's website for details).  You can also take the train from Central to Blacktown Station (the trip takes about 35 to 45 minutes).  From there it's easiest to catch a cab or an Uber.  That trip takes about 5 minutes.  If you're on a strict budget bus number 729, departing from Blacktown Station, Stand F, will take you there in 10 minutes.

Opening hours: 8.00 am to 5.00 pm seven days.

Time budget:  At least three hours, five if you're traveling from the CBD but it's pretty much an all-day commitment.

How much:  Prices start from as $22 per person.  You can also arrange for a Personal Koala Encounter for an additional fee.

While you're in the area:  If it's really warm weather and you have plenty of time and energy left over, you can spend some time at **Raging Waters** (see opposite).

## Raging Waters

Why you should go:  Because it's arguably Sydney's premier water park (formerly Wet 'n' Wild) and a great way for a family to spend a long, hot day.  Note:  It's only open during the warmer months and it really pays to plan this trip in advance.

Address: 427 Reservoir Road, Prospect 2148

Phone: 139 697

Website: **www.ragingwaterssydney.com.au**

How to get there:  Raging Waters is a long way from the CBD and the quickest and easiest way to get there is by car.  Otherwise, you can take the train from Central to Blacktown Station (the trip takes about 35 to 45 minutes).  From there it's easiest to catch a cab or an Uber.  That trip takes about 15 minutes.

Opening hours:  Variable, check the website first.

Time budget:  It's a whole day trip, unless you have a lot of time and energy and you can squeeze in a visit, preferably first, to **Featherdale Wildlife Park** (see opposite).

How much:  Pass prices are variable and change every year.  It's worth checking out various discounts on the internet.  For example, NRMA members can get a pass at a substantial discount.  The deals are out there if you look for them.

## Blue Mountains

Why you should go: Because there are more than a million hectares of World Heritage listed bushland within easy access of Sydney and in excess of 140 kilometres (85 miles) of walking trails with stunning views across the valleys. The Blue Mountains is also home to charming villages and a thriving artistic community. For those with only a short time to spend in the mountains, the best place to start is the village of **Katoomba** with the famous **Three Sisters** rock formation and **Scenic World** with its skyway, cable car and train rides (**www.scenicworld.com.au**).

Website: **www.visitbluemountains.com.au**

How to get there: There are many tour groups with day trips from the CBD to the Blue Mountains. Trains from Central depart hourly and take two hours. Scenic World is 3 kilometres/less than 2 miles from Katoomba train station and visitors can take the hop-on hop-off Blue Mountains Explorer bus or the 686 bus.

Time budget: It's at least a whole day trip. Also consider the remarkable **Jenolan Caves** (**www.jenolancaves.org.au**).

## Gourmet Food Safaris

Exploring Sydney's different food cultures is a delicious way to experience Sydney's diversity and see how the locals really live. Tours include Vietnamese food in Cabramatta, Lebanese in Punchbowl, Turkish in Auburn and Greek in Marrickville.

Phone: 02 8969 6555; Website: **www.gourmetsafaris.com.au**.

Sydney is famous for a number of events that only happen once a year (listed here in calendar order) and you can plan your visit around them.  Many of the event websites offer you the opportunity to go on an email list so that they can notify you as soon as dates and specific events are finalized.

# Once a Year if You Can Make It

## Sydney Festival

Sydney gets the new year off to a month-long program of cultural events all over the city that take place throughout January. The program includes major and emerging international and Australian acts. Overseas visitors should note that the whole of January is summer school holiday time in Australia.

Website: **www.sydneyfestival.org.au**

## Sydney Gay and Lesbian Mardi Gras

The Mardi Gras is an internationally renowned event that culminates with a joyous and spectacular parade up Oxford Street from the city celebrating the identity and culture of the queer community, bringing visitors from all over the world. It's usually held in late February or early March.

Website: **www.mardigras.org.au**

## Sydney Royal Easter Show

The show began as an agricultural show in 1823 and is now Australia's largest ticketed event. Since its inception it has broadened its brief to become '… a celebration of Australian culture, from our rural traditions to our modern-day lifestyles …' It's usually held around early April for two weeks at **Sydney Showground at Olympic Park** and includes everything from judging of animals and produce to sideshow alley with rides, showbags and fun for all the family.

Website: **www.eastershow.com.au**

Sydney Town Hall
during Vivid Sydney

# Sydney Writers' Festival

The writers' festival is a week-or-so-long collection of literary events showcasing books and writers from all over the world. The festival hub is at **Carriageworks** (page 88) but there are events at venues around Sydney; some are free, some are paid. For all those who love the written word. It's usually held in late April, early May.

Website: **www.swf.org.au**

# Australian Heritage Festival

Begun in 1980 by the National Trust, the festival is a month-long collection of events all over Australia celebrating the country and its history. The festival is an opportunity to access places and buildings that are generally not open to the public at other times. It's usually held from mid-April to mid-May.

Website: **www.nationaltrust.org.au/ahf**

# Vivid Sydney

As the months grow colder and the days get darker Sydney compensates by putting on a festival of light, music and ideas. Although it's principally known as an opportunity to use the latest technology to paint buildings with laser beams, there's also a lot more to it than that with the music program attracting some of the world's best artists to perform at venues including the **Sydney Opera House** and **Carriageworks.** The installations around Circular Quay, the Opera House and Royal Botanic Gardens attract huge crowds so it is advisable to try and go earlier in the week. Usually held in late May.

Website: **www.vividsydney.com**

## Sydney Film Festival

The two-week-long Sydney Film Festival, a celebration of all things cinematic, is usually held in early June. Website: **www.sff.org.au**

## Whale Festival

For one day in early October celebrate Aboriginal heritage and the annual *gawura* (whale) migration season. It's free, but you need to register. Website: **www.sydneylivingmuseums.com.au**

## Sculpture by the Sea

The largest outdoor showcase of sculpture in Australia by local and international artists is held in Sydney along the coastline from **Bondi Beach** (page 104) to **Tamarama Beach** for three weeks from late-October to mid-November. It's free and is hugely popular on weekends so it's best to go early in the week if you can.

Website: **www.sculpturebythesea.com/bondi**

## Sydney to Hobart Yacht Race

This annual yacht race has been held since 1945 and attracts huge crowds around **Sydney Harbour** on Boxing Day (26 December) to watch the start of the race.

Website: **www.rolexsydneyhobart.com**

## Sydney New Year's Eve

The Sydney year ends with SydNYE, the annual New Year's Eve fireworks where a city of millions, hundreds of thousands of visitors and a TV audience of 1 billion cast their gaze to a show on Sydney Harbour like no other. Website: **www.sydneynewyearseve.com**

# Eateries and Drinkeries

Obviously, you're going to have to eat and drink at some point and where and what will depend on your whims, moods and, literally, your tastes. You can find food from virtually anywhere in the world in Sydney, with different cultural communities established and thriving across the city.

Naturally, restaurants often change their menus and even their opening times depending on season and time of the year, so we can only offer an approximate idea of highly recommended venues and it's best to check their website for their current status. Here's a selection of suggestions.

# Food with a View

The following restaurants not only have great food, but stunning views as well that come at no extra charge.

## The Bathers' Pavilion

4 The Esplanade, Balmoral 2088
Restaurant open for lunch 12.00 pm to 2.30 pm Wednesday
  to Sunday, dinner 6.30 pm to 9 pm Wednesday to Saturday;
  cafe open 7 am to 10.30 pm seven days
Phone: 02 9969 5050
Website: **www.batherspavilion.com.au/restaurant**
Known for:  French with a twist.

## The Boathouse on Blackwattle Bay

123 Ferry Road, Glebe 2037
Open for lunch 12.00 pm to 2:45 pm Friday to Sunday, dinner
  from 6.00 pm Tuesday to Sunday;  brunch from 10.00 am to
  12.00 pm every Sunday
Phone: 02 9518 9011
Website: **www.boathouse.net.au**
Known for:  Seafood.

## Catalina Restaurant

Lyne Park, Rose Bay 2029
Open for lunch from 12.00 pm seven days,
  dinner Monday to Saturday from 6.00 pm
Phone: 02 9371 0555
Website: **www.catalinarosebay.com.au**
Known for:  Up-market modern Australian, seafood.

## Doyles on the Beach

11 Marine Parade, Watsons Bay 2047 (GPS address, 3 Cliff Street)

Open for lunch 12.00 pm to 3.00 pm Monday to Friday, to
   4.00 pm on Saturday and Sunday, dinner Sunday to Thursday
   5.30 pm to 8.30 pm, to 9.00 pm Friday to Saturday.

Phone: 02 9377 2007

Website: **www.doyles.com.au**

Known for: Seafood. They also have a takeaway service, **Doyles
on the Wharf**, open from 10.00 am to 5.00 pm every day.

## Hugos Manly

Shop 1, Manly Wharf, East Esplanade, Manly 2095

Open for lunch and dinner from 12.00 pm to late Monday to
   Friday and from 11.30 am to late on Saturday and Sunday

Phone: 02 8116 8555

Website: **www.hugos.com.au**

Known for: Modern Italian, pizza.

## Icebergs Dining Room and Bar

1 Notts Avenue, Bondi Beach 2026

Open for lunch from 12.00 pm seven days, dinner from 6.30 pm
   seven days, brunch 10.00 am to 12.00 pm every Sunday

Phone: 02 9365 9000

Website: **www.idrb.com**

Known for: Seasonal modern Italian.

## Ormeggio at the Spit

D'Albora Marinas, Spit Road, Mosman 2088

Open for lunch from 11:45 am Friday to Sunday;  dinner from
    5:45 pm Wednesday to Saturday, from 6.30 pm on Sunday

Phone: 02 9969 4088

Website: **www.ormeggio.com.au**

Known for:  Modern Italian cuisine.

## The Pantry

Ocean Promenade, North Steyne 2095

Open for breakfast 7.30 am to 11.30 am seven days, lunch
    and dinner from 12.00 pm to late seven days

Phone: 02 9977 0566

Website: **www.thepantrymanly.com**

Known for:  Local and seasonal modern Australian, seafood.

## Quay Restaurant

Overseas Passenger Terminal, Circular Quay, Sydney 2000

Open for lunch from 12.00 pm to 1.30 pm Friday to Sunday,
    dinner 6.00 pm to 9.30 pm daily

Phone: 02 9251 5600

Website: **www.quay.com.au**

Known for:  One of the country's most celebrated modern
    Australian restaurants with views across Circular Quay to
    the Sydney Opera House.

## Ripples Milsons Point

Olympic Drive, Milsons Point 2061

Open for breakfast 8.00 am to 10.30 am Monday to Friday,
7.30 am to 10.30 am weekends, lunch from 12.00 pm seven
days, dinner from 6.00 pm seven days

Phone: 02 9929 7722

Website: **www.ripplesmilsonspoint.com.au**

Known for: Modern Italian cuisine.

## Fine Dining

Some of these places also have wonderful views, but for the most
part Sydneysiders-in-the-know also consider them to be among the
best restaurants in the city.

## Aqua Dining

Corner of Northcliff Street and Paul Street, Milsons Point 2061

Open for lunch from 12.00 pm, dinner from 6.00 pm, seven days

Phone: 02 9964 9998

Website: **www.aquadining.com.au**

Known for: Contemporary Italian cuisine.

## Aria Restaurant Sydney

1 Macquarie Street, Sydney 2000

Open for lunch from 12.00 pm to 2.15 pm weekdays, to 1.30 pm
Saturdays, to 1:45 pm Sundays, dinner from 5.30 pm to
10.30 pm weekdays and Sundays, to 11.00 pm Saturdays

Phone: 02 9240 2255

Website: **www.ariasydney.com.au**

Known for: Modern Australian haute cuisine.

## Bea Restaurant

Barangaroo House, 1/35 Barangaroo Avenue, Barangaroo 2000

Open for lunch from 12.00 pm to 3.00 pm seven days, dinner
  5.30 pm to 12.00 am seven days

Phone: 02 8587 5400

Website: **www.barangaroohouse.com.au/bea-food-menu**

Known for: Hearty seasonal contemporary Australian cuisine.

## Bennelong

Sydney Opera House, Bennelong Point 2000

Open for lunch from 12.00 pm seven days; dinner from 5.30 pm
  seven days

Phone: 02 9240 8000

Website: **www.bennelong.com.au**

Known for: Produce-driven modern Australian with spectacular
  architecture and views. Also check out the **Opera Kitchen** on
  the Lower Concourse Level for casual dining. Open for breakfast,
  lunch and dinner from 7:30 till late seven days.

## Blue Eye Dragon

37 Pyrmont Street, Pyrmont 2009

Open for lunch and dinner 12.00 pm to 9.00 pm weekdays but
  serving only small plates from 2.30 pm to 5.30 pm, dinner
  5.30 pm to 9.00 pm Saturdays

Phone: 02 9964 9998

Website: **www.blueeyedragon.com.au**

Known for: Taiwanese cuisine.

## Cafe Sydney

Fifth floor, Customs House, 31 Alfred Street, Sydney 2000
Open for lunch and dinner 12.00 pm to late Monday to Saturday,
   open for lunch only from 12.00 pm on Sundays
Phone: 02 9251 8683
Website: **www.cafesydney.com**
Known for:  Modern Australian cuisine, seafood.

## China Doll

4/6 Cowper Wharf Road, Woolloomooloo 2011
Open for lunch from 12.00 pm and for dinner from 6.00 pm
   seven days
Phone: 02 9380 6744
Website: **www.chinadoll.com.au**
Known for:  Up-market pan-Asian cuisine and cocktails.

## est.

Level 1/252 George Street, Sydney 2000
Open for lunch 12.00 pm to 2.30 pm Monday to Friday, dinner
   6.00 pm to 10.00 pm Monday to Saturday
Phone: 02 9114 7312
Website: **www.merivale.com/venues/est**
Known for:  Contemporary Australian fine dining with an extensive
   wine list.

## Golden Century Seafood Restaurant

393–399 Sussex Street, Sydney 2000
Open for lunch and dinner 12.00 pm to 4.00 am seven days
Phone: 02 9212 3901
Website: **www.goldencentury.com.au**

Known for:  Simple decor but great Chinese seafood including live
   lobsters in glass tanks – it doesn't get any fresher.

## Mr Wong

3 Bridge Lane, Sydney 2000
Open for lunch 12.00 pm to 3.00 pm Monday to Friday and from
   10.30 am weekends, dinner from 5.30 pm seven days
Phone: 02 9114 7317
Website: **www.merivale.com/venues/mrwong**
Known for:  Contemporary Chinese and dim sum (lunch only).

## Rockpool Bar & Grill

66 Hunter Street, Sydney 2000
Open for lunch from 12.00 pm to 3.00 pm Monday to Friday,
   dinner from 6.00 pm Monday to Friday and Sunday, from
   5.30 pm Saturday
Phone: 02 8099 7077
Website: **www.rockpoolbarandgrill.com.au**
Known for:  Steak and seafood in one of Australia's most beautiful
   dining rooms.

## Tetsuya's Restaurant

529 Kent Street, Sydney 2000
Open for lunch from 12.00 pm Saturday only, dinner from 5.30 pm
   Tuesday to Friday and from 6.30 pm Saturday
Phone: 02 9267 2900
Website: **www.tetsuyas.com**
Known for:  Japanese-French fusion cuisine and a degustation
   menu that changes with the seasons, overlooking a serene
   Japanese garden.

# Food Experiences You Have to Try

Not all extraordinary food experiences are defined just by the food or the view.  Sometimes it's the context or the venue.

## *360 Bar and Dining/Sydney Tower Buffet*

Sydney Tower, Castlereagh Street, Sydney 2000
Sydney's revolving restaurants are few.  The 360 Bar is 250 meters (800 feet) above street level with panoramic views and a buffet.
Open: 360 Bar and Dining open for lunch from 12.00 pm to 4.00 pm seven days, dinner from 5.30 pm seven days (last seating at 9.00 pm);  buffet lunch 11.30 am to 3.30 pm seven days (last seating 2.00pm), buffet dinner from 5.00 pm seven days (last seating 9.00pm)
Phone: 02 8223 38883
Website: **www.360dining.com.au**

## The Bush Food Experience
## at the Royal Botanic Gardens

A real eye-opener about Indigenous dining and how to incorporate native Australian ingredients into your own cooking. From 1.00 pm to 3.00 pm once a month on the grounds of the gardens, $85 per person. Bookings essential.

Website: **www.rbgsyd.nsw.gov.au/whatson/ aboriginal-bush-food-experience**

## Munich Brauhaus

33 Playfair Street, The Rocks 2000

A slice of Bavaria that seems to have found a permanent home in Sydney. It's like having Oktoberfest every day of the year.

Open: 11.00 am to late Monday to Friday, 9.00 am to late on weekends

Phone: 02 9958 2910

Website: **www.thebavarians.com**

## Kensington Street and Spice Alley

Kensington Street, Chippendale 2008

Kensington Street and the adjacent Spice Alley is a mini-district entirely dedicated to eating, drinking, street food and shopping. The sheer range of venues in such a small space is almost overwhelming and is divided into four mini-mini districts: Spice Alley, The Old Rum Store, Eastside and Westside.

Open: hours vary between venues

Website: **www.kensingtonstreet.com.au/all-vendors**

# Pub Dining

There's only so much haute cuisine, restaurants with stunning views, or quirky, offbeat eateries that you can take. Sometimes you just want a simple, pub meal, and it's at a pub that you can get an opportunity to mix with the locals. The Australian pub, a tradition inherited from the UK, has taken on a particular Australian character all its own and is a genuine Australian institution that comes in many shapes and sizes. There are some parts of inner Sydney that are particularly known for the number of interesting pubs including **The Rocks,** Balmain, Surry Hills and Paddington.

## *The Balmain Hotel*

72–76 Mullins Street, Balmain 2041

Open: 12.00 pm to midnight Monday to Saturday, to 10.00 pm
  Sunday

Phone: 02 9810 7500

Website: **www.thebalmain.com**

Known for:  A 'gourmet' pub with a kitschy interior and an open
  courtyard.  Walk north up Mullins Street and you'll be in the
  heart of Balmain, one of Sydney's more colorful suburbs.

## *The Courthouse Hotel*

202 Australia Street, Newtown 2042

Open: 10.00 am to midnight Monday to Saturday, to 10.00 pm
  Sunday

Phone: 02 9114 7317

Website: **www.solotel.com.au/venue-details/pub/courthouse-hotel**

Known for:  Being a laid-back, informal, country-style place with a
  nice courtyard.  Known to the locals as 'The Courty'.

## The Harbour View Hotel

18 Lower Fort Street, Dawes Point 2000

Open: 11.00 am to midnight Monday to Saturday, 10.00 pm
Sunday

Phone: 02 9252 4111

Website: **www.harbourview.com.au**

Known for: Upscale pub dining, plus a rooftop cocktail bar with
Harbour Bridge views.

## The Glenmore Hotel

96 Cumberland Street, The Rocks 2000

Open: 11.00 am to midnight Sunday to Thursday, to 1.00 am
Friday and Saturday

Phone: 02 9247 4794

Website: **www.theglenmore.com.au**

Known for: Founded in 1921, a gourmet pub on three levels with
restaurant, cocktail bar, a rooftop level and harbor views.

## The Hero of Waterloo

81 Lower Fort Street, Millers Point 2000

Open: 11.00 am to 11.30 pm Monday to Wednesday, to midnight
Thursday to Saturday, to 10.00 pm Sunday

Phone: 02 9252 4553

Website: **www.heroofwaterloo.com.au**

Known for: Being in a building that looks as if it was built by
convicts (because it was!). Also has ghost tours and live bands,
not necessarily in that order.

## The Lord Nelson Brewery Hotel

19 Kent Street, The Rocks 2000

Open: 11.00 am to 11.00 pm Monday to Saturday, 12.00 pm
  to 10.00 pm Sunday;  restaurant open for lunch 12.00 pm to
  3.00 pm Thursday and Friday, dinner 6.00 pm to 10.00 pm
  Tuesday to Saturday

Phone: 02 9251 4044

Website: **www.lordnelsonbrewery.com**

Known for:  Being Sydney's oldest continuously licensed hotel and
  also Australia's oldest pub brewery, established in 1841.  The
  craft beers have won awards, the food is well regarded and you
  can stay there too.

## The Oaks Hotel

118 Military Road, Neutral Bay 2089

Open: 10.00 am to midnight Monday to Thursday, 10.00 am to
  1.30 am Friday and Saturday, 12.00 pm to midnight Sunday

Phone Number: 02 9953 5515

Website: **www.oakshotel.com.au**

Known for:  Upscale 'pub grub' served in an interior with a retro
  decor.  You can even cook your own steak and there's a leafy
  patio for hot days.

## The Tilbury Hotel

12–18 Nicholson Street, Woolloomooloo 2011

Open: 11.00 am to 10.00 pm Sunday to Thursday, to midnight
  Friday and Saturday

Phone: 02 9953 5515

Website: **www.tilburyhotel.com.au**

Known for:  Light and bright newly renovated dining space with gastropub meals and an outdoor courtyard.

## The Unicorn Hotel

106 Oxford Street, Paddington

Open: 4.00 pm to 1.00 am Monday and Tuesday, 4.00 pm to 3.00 am Wednesday, 11.00 am to 3.00 am Thursday to Saturday, 11.00 am to midnight Sunday

Phone Number: 02 9953 5515

Website: **www.theunicornhotel.com.au**

Known for:  Its Art Deco interior and nostalgic Australian bistro meals, live music.  Definitely a place for night owls.

## The Welcome Hotel

91 Evans Street, Rozelle 2039

Open: 11.30 am to midnight Monday to Saturday, 12.00 pm to 10.00 pm Sunday.

Phone: 02 9810 1323

Website: **www.thewelcomehotel.com.au**

Known for:  Italian-inspired food and craft beers in an 1890s pub with a leafy beer garden.

## The Woolloomooloo Bay Hotel

2 Bourke Road, Woolloomooloo 2011

Open: 10.00 am to midnight Monday to Saturday, to 10.00 pm Sunday.

Phone: 02 9357 1177

Website: **www.woolloomooloobayhotel.com.au**

Known for:  Upscale bistro-type meals, Australian cuisine and premium steaks.

# Drinks with a View and the Best Rooftop Bars

If you need to take a break in the middle of the day from all the pleasures of Sydney, or after a hard day's treading the pavements, you might just want to park yourself somewhere nice and have a drink or two.

## Café del Mar

Rooftop Terrace, Cockle Bay Wharf, 35 Wheat Road, Sydney 2000
Open: 12.00 pm to late Tuesday to Sunday
Phone: 02 9267 6700
Website: **www.cafedelmar.com.au**
Known for:  A Mediterranean restaurant with an outdoor terrace and views of Darling Harbour.

## The Glasshouse at the Hotel Steyne, Manly

75 The Corso, Manly 2095
Open: 4.00 pm to 11.00 pm Thursday and Friday, 11.00 am to 11.00 pm Saturday, 11.00 am to 10.00 pm Sunday
Phone: 02 9977 4977
Website: **www.hotelsteyne.com.au/glasshouse**
Known for:  Its view of the Pacific Ocean looking out from one of Manly's oldest buildings, built in 1936 and now heritage listed.

## Ivy Pool Club

Level 4, 320 George Street, Sydney 2000
Open: 12.00 pm to late Wednesday to Friday, 6.00 pm to late Saturday
Phone: 02 9114 7307
Website: **www.merivale.com/venues/poolclub**

Known for: Its casual, relaxed, poolside ambience – it's like being at a resort.

## *O Bar and Dining*

Level 47, Australia Square, 264 George Street, Sydney 2000
Open: 12.00 pm to late seven days
Phone: 02 9247 9777
Website: **www.obardining.com.au/lounge-bar**
Known for: It's amazing views from Australia Square and huge range of spirits.

## *Old Mate's Place*

Level 4, 199 Clarence Street, Sydney 2000
Open: 5.00 pm to 2.00 am Tuesday and Wednesday, 12.00 pm to 2.00 am Thursday to Saturday, 2.00 pm to 2.00 am Sunday
Phone: It's a secret and they don't take bookings. You just wander in.
Website: **www.oldmates.sydney**
Known for: Hard-to-find and therefore exclusive with an amazing collection of spirits and liqueurs in an old-world ambience. Really unique.

## *Smoke Bar*

Level 2, 35 Barangaroo Avenue, Barangaroo 2000
Open: 3.00 pm to midnight Monday to Thursday, 12.00 pm to midnight Friday to Sunday
Phone: 02 8587 5400
Website: **www.barangaroohouse.com.au/smoke-bar-menu**
Known for: Unusual architecture and high-end pub grub.

## Zeta Bar

Level 4, 88 George Street, Sydney 2000 (inside the Hilton Hotel)

Open: 5.00 pm to midnight Monday to Thursday, 5.00 pm to
2.00 am Friday 5.00 pm to 3.00 am Saturday

Phone: 02 9265 6070

Website: **www.zetabar.com.au**

Known for: Its unusual and eclectic interior design and great view
of the **Queen Victoria Building** which is just opposite. Particularly
nice at night. See also **The Marble Bar** (page 152).

# Wining and Whiskeying

## Gallon

117 Harris Street, Pyrmont 2009

Open: 12.00 pm to midnight Tuesday to Friday, 1.00 pm
to midnight Saturday, 1.00 pm to 10 pm Sunday

Phone: 0402 799 557

Website: **www.galllon.com.au**

Known for: Local and international wine and beer, hearty pizzas
and small plates and a leafy courtyard.

## GPO Cheese and Wine Room

GPO Building, Lower Ground Floor, 1 Martin Place, Sydney 2000

Open: Lunch 12.00 pm to 3.00 pm Tuesday to Friday, dinner
6.00 pm to 10.00 pm Tuesday to Saturday

Phone: 02 9229 7701

Website: **www.gpogrand.com/gpo-best-cheese-wine-room-sydney**

Known for: Fondue, antipasti and tasting plates in a stylish
European-style space.

## Shady Pines Saloon

4/256 Crown Street, Darlinghurst 2010

Open: 4.00 pm to midnight seven days

Phone: 0405 624 944

Website: **www.shadypinessaloon.com**

Known for: About as close as you'll get to being in the Wild West if you happen to be in Sydney. It's well known for its whiskey – as well as its sarsaparilla and peanut snacks.

## Sokyo Lounge

Level G, The Star, 80 Pyrmont Street, Pyrmont 2009

Open: 5.30 pm to 10.00 pm Sunday to Thursday, to 10.30 pm Friday and Saturday

Phone: 1800 700 700

Website: **www.star.com.au/sydney/eat-and-drink/signature-dining/sokyo**

Known for: Japanese-inspired cocktails and a large sake list.

## ArtHouse

275 Pitt Street, Sydney 2000

Open: 10.00 am to midnight Monday to Wednesday, to 1.30 am Thursday, to 3.00 am Friday, to 3.30 am Saturday

Phone: 02 9284 1200

Website: **www.arthousehotel.com.au/spaces**

Known for: Being many venues in one, including Graffiti Wine Lounge, Attic cocktail bar and the VIP Lounge, all set in a former art school dating from 1836.

## The Baxter Inn

152–156 Clarence Street, Sydney 2000

Open: 4.00 pm to 1.00 am seven days

Phone: It's a secret. Just show up. They don't take bookings.

Website: **www.thebaxterinn.com**

Known for: A sophisticated and rather exclusive bar with its own special feel, featuring an extensive selection of top-shelf whiskies and classic cocktails.

## The Dolphin Hotel

412 Crown Street, Surry Hills 2010

Open: 11.30 am to 12.00 am Monday to Saturday, 11.30 am to 10.00 pm Sunday

Phone: 02 9331 4800

Website: **www.dolphinhotel.com.au**

Known for: Across three levels, with a light, breezy feel, including an outdoor terrace. The Wine Room features 35 carefully selected wines by the glass with a menu to match.

## Marble Bar

Level B1, 488 George Street, Sydney 2000

Open: 3.30 pm to midnight Sunday to Thursday, to 2.00 am Friday, to 3.00 am Saturday

Phone: 02 9266 2000

Website: **www.marblebarsydney.com.au**

Known for: Extraordinary Victorian decor and for its selection of wine and spirits. See also **Zeta Bar** (page 150).

## The Roosevelt

32 Orwell Street, Potts Point 2011

Open: 5.00 pm to midnight Monday to Friday, 3.00 pm to
midnight Saturday, 12.00 pm to 10.00 pm Sunday

Phone: 0423 203 119

Website: **www.threroosevelt.com.au**

Known for: About as close to being in a sophisticated New York
bar while in Sydney. It even has a private poker den.

## Wine Library

18 Oxford Street, Woollahra 2025

Open: 4.00 pm to midnight Monday to Thursday, 12.00 pm to
midnight Friday and Saturday, 12.00 pm to 10.00 pm Sunday

Phone: 02 9368 7484

Website: **www.wine-library.com.au**

Known for: A cozy bar with a wide and interesting selection of
wines and a menu to match.

## The Winery

285A Crown Street, Surry Hills 2010

Open: 12.00 pm to midnight seven days

Phone: 02 8322 2007

Website: **www.thewinerysurryhills.com.au**

Known for: A quirky urban garden oasis in the heart of Surry Hills
with more than 30 wines by the glass and sophisticated, yet
relaxed, dining.

# Beers and Spirits

## *All Hands Brewing House*

22 The Promenade, Sydney 2000

Open: 11.00 am to late seven days

Phone: 02 8270 7901

Website: **www.allhandsbrewinghouse.com.au**

Known for:  Located in Darling Harbour with a state-of-the-art microbrewery, Southern-style comfort menu, and a beer garden on the wharf.

## *Endeavour Tap Rooms*

39–43 Argyle Street, The Rocks 2000

Open: 11.00 am to midnight Monday to Saturday, to 10.00 pm Sunday

Phone: 02 9241 6517

Website: **www.taprooms.com.au**

Known for:  Craft beers and smoked and barbecue meats in a cozy historic bar.

## *Kittyhawk*

16 Phillip Lane, Sydney 2000

Open: 3.00 pm to midnight Monday to Friday, 4.00 pm to midnight Saturday

Phone:  It's a secret.  Contact them via their website.

Website: **www.thekittyhawk.com.au**

Known for:  A French restaurant and cocktail bar inspired by the Liberation of Paris in 1944.  The cocktails are 'exceptional' – if they do say so themselves.

## THE MARRICKVILLE BREWERIES AND STORES

For reasons that remain obscure there's a whole cluster of craft beer microbreweries in the former industrial suburb of Marrickville, which isn't all that far from the CBD. And all these breweries are within an easy walk of each other.

Opening hours vary according to the breweries. Best to check ahead for each one so you can plan your own microbrewery tour of Sydney. Below is a convenient list with a recommended visiting order. Be sure to take along some hefty bags or get your hands on a trolley if you plan to buy lots of bottles. To get there, take the train from Central to Marrickville Station, a 15-minute trip. Then walk north up the left side of Illawarra Road until you reach:

**Bucket Boys Craft Beer Co.** 300 Illawarra Road; Phone: 0431 614 578; Website:**www.bucketboys.com.au**

**Batch Brewing Company** 44 Sydenham Road; Phone: 02 9550 5432; Website: **www.batchbrewingco.com.au**

**Stockade Brew Co.** 25 Cadogan Street; Phone: 024606 1016; Website: **www.stockadebrewco.com.au**

**Sauce Brewing Co.** 1a Mitchell Street; Phone: 02 8580 3555; Website: **www.sauce.beer**

**Wildflower Brewing & Blending** 11–13 Brompton Street; no phone; Website: **www.wildflowerbeer.com**

**The Grifter Brewing Co.** 391–397 Enmore Road; Phone: 02 9550 5742; Website: **www.thegrifter.com.au**

Once you've completed your tour keep going further north along Enmore Road. Eventually Enmore Road veers right and east and you'll reach Enmore, which is an interesting suburb with vintage fashion and small bars. Keep going east along Enmore Road and you'll reach Newtown, which is known for its many independent shops, cafes, bars and restaurants and is a great place to have a wander.

## Pumphouse Bar & Restaurant

17 Little Pier Street, Darling Harbour 2000

Open: 12.00 pm to 10.00 pm seven days

Phone: 02 8217 4100

Website: **www.pumphousesydney.com.au**

Known for: Its extensive list of craft, rare and seasonal beers and
hearty food offerings.

## Quarryman's Hotel

214–216 Harris Street, Pyrmont 2009

Open: 11.00 am to midnight Monday to Saturday, to 10.00 pm
   Sunday;  rooftop open 12.00 pm to late Wednesday to Sunday

Phone: 02 9660 0560

Website: **www.quarrymans.com.au**

Known for:  Light, airy feel, more than 20 craft beers on tap,
   a hearty menu and rooftop terrace.

## Redoak Boutique Beer Cafe

201 Clarence Street, Sydney 2000

Open: 12.00 pm to 11.00 pm Monday to Wednesday, to midnight
   Thursday to Saturday

Phone: 02 9262 3303

Website: **www.redoak.com.au**

Known for:  One of the original craft breweries, specializing in
   European-style beers and a menu with suggested beer matches.

## The Taphouse

122 Flinders Street, Darlinghurst 2010

Open: 12.00 pm to midnight Monday to Thursday, to 1.00 am
   Friday and Saturday, to 11.00 pm Sunday

Phone: 02 9360 0088

Website: **www.taphousedarlo.com.au**

Known for:  Showcasing a diverse range of local, independently
   owned beers over 60 taps.  There's also a wine list with a great
   range of Australian natural wines and artisanal spirits.

# Coffee

Sydneysiders love their coffee, with migrants from Greece and Italy bringing their coffee traditions with them after the Second World War. The quality of coffee is high almost anywhere you go but many locals will travel across town for the perfect cup or their favorite barista (coffee maker/magician). Here are a few to seek out:

### Brewtown Newtown

6–9 O'Connell Street, Newtown 2042

### Edition Coffee Roasters

60 Darling Drive, Haymarket 2000

### Gumption

The Strand Arcade, Sydney 2000

### Pablo and Rusty's

161 Castlereagh Street, Sydney 2000

### Paramount Coffee Project

80 Commonwealth Street, Surry Hills 2010

### Regiment

Ground Floor, 333 George Street, Sydney 2000

### Reuben Hills

61 Albion Street, Surry Hills 2010

### Single O

60–64 Reservoir Street, Surry Hills 2010
89 York Street, Sydney 2000

The Strand Arcade

First published in 2019 by New Holland Publishers
London • Sydney • Auckland

Bentinck House, 3–8 Bolsover Street, London W1W 6AB, UK
1/66 Gibbes Street, Chatswood, NSW 2067, Australia
5/39 Woodside Ave, Northcote, Auckland 0627, New Zealand

newhollandpublishers.com

A record of this book is held at the British Library and the National Library of Australia.

ISBN 9781760791322

Group Managing Director: Fiona Schultz
Author: Xavier Waterkeyn
Project Editor: Liz Hardy
Designer: Andrew Davies
Production Director: Arlene Gippert
Printer: Toppan Leefung Printing Limited

10 9 8 7 6 5 4 3 2 1

Keep up with New Holland Publishers:
NewHollandPublishers
@newhollandpublishers